Zen Dust

For Charles
with best wishes

Zen Dust

A journey home through the
back roads of South Africa

by Antony Osler

JACANA

Published by Jacana Media (Pty) Ltd in 2012
Second impression 2016

10 Orange Street
Sunnyside
Auckland Park 2092
South Africa
+2711 628 3200
www.jacana.co.za

ISBN 978-1-4314-0617-3

Poem on page xv from the *Book of Serenity*, case 92
Poem on page 134 from *The Wind One Brilliant Day*
    by Antonio Machado, translated by Robert Bly
All poems by the author, some adapted from traditional sources
Cover design by Maggie Davey and Shawn Paikin
Set in Didot 10/15pt
Printed and bound by ABC Press, Cape Town
Job No. 002908

See a complete list of Jacana titles at www.jacana.co.za

to Margie
who walked with me every step of this wonderful path;
and who can smell humbug a mile off

THANKS

I am so grateful to have had the privilege of writing this book that I wanted to thank all beings everywhere. My editor has asked me to limit that a little so let me begin with her. Jacqui L'Ange has responded to the text with all her heart and successfully resisted all my attempts at improving it to death. My dear friends Bridget Impey and Maggie Davey of Jacana have once again believed in the book and encouraged me to make it more than merely a sequel to *Stoep Zen*. Maggie, Kerrie Barlow and Shawn Paiken brought all their astonishing skill and enthusiasm to the design. And the whole Jacana team looked after Margie and myself in Johannesburg when the big city left us bewildered. During it all, my family helped keep me afloat – Margie my wife, to whom this book is dedicated; daughters Emma and Sarah who have turned out to be such interesting and affectionate adults; my siblings and their spouses, Maeder and Les Osler, Marguerite and Charles van der Merwe. And, as always, Louis and Chrisi van Loon were there to cheer from the sidelines.

So many people have contributed to the text in one way or another, often unbeknown to themselves. I want to thank particularly Dolf Schutte, Norman Coates, Maeder Osler, Mervyn Croft, Tessa Pretorius, Thandi Gaqa, JC van der Merwe, Johan Sheffer, Simon Cashmore,

Kevin Shoulder and Shiraz Osman. Our sangha at Poplar Grove, as well as our Dharma friends at Furnace Mountain, Emoyeni and the Buddhist Retreat Centre, provided endless inspiration and endured my tentative readings on retreat.

The photographs are an integral part of the book and I must bow first to David Collett, who gave up so many hours of his precious retirement to take photos as well as to edit and co-ordinate pictures for the book; his generosity has been without reserve. Thank you, David. Apart from photos by David and myself, many other friends responded to the call for material; Graeme Williams, Albe Grobbelaar, Ant Rissik, Marie-Louise Steyn, Annelize Bertalan, Leslie Goodman, Gerrit Du Preez, Ollie Schafer and Lisa Buerkle all allowed me to use their beautiful photos. On page 132 there is a photo of a basin at Poplar Grove with a framed painting of the same basin on the wall above it; the original painting is by Andries Gouws and is included here by his kind permission. The cover photo is by David Collett.

And, finally, I present this book to my Zen teacher Dae Gak Zen Master of Furnace Mountain, who has re-awakened my commitment to finding a clear and heartfelt way through this life and who generously created and donated the stunning original calligraphies for the book.

INTRODUCTION

So I ask myself what kind of book I want to write. If I listen carefully enough I already know. It is the book where I can feel my heart opening. Something that allows me to sigh or stand a little straighter, Aah Yes!... little surprises, gifts, somersaults. Even a tear or two. Not dramatic epiphanies, not finding ourselves on our knees between the bookshelves, but small bells of aliveness that ring as we turn the pages.

Such moments are important. They are the beads on which we thread our life, clear and spontaneous in a way that our normal thought-filled life seldom is. And they are delicate, hardly there at all, impossible to see if we look too hard. Like having a small child in the bed and waking with the sense of something precious at your side. Easily crushed by too much thinking. For they are moments of innocence, of openness, of delicate selfless attention. Awakeness.

Buddhism is a tradition of awakening. But awakening is not just Buddhist, it is everywhere. For this is the taste of life itself. The tone and style of this book are those of Zen Buddhism – not because it is a better way but because it is the way I know. And the setting is wherever my own steps have taken me – South Africa where I live, North America, the United Kingdom, East Asia. May it speak to all people everywhere, of every religious persuasion and none. It is written from the heart as a rambling journey, out of my own rambling journey. May it speak to you.

There is another mark of the kind of book that I want to read. I want to be 'fetched' – to use the wonderful phrase of Joan Sutherland Roshi. I want to read words that call me beyond myself into an aliveness just out of reach. Pointing words. Come, they say, come look here! Poems and paintings can be like that, or a tender piece of cabinet-making that stirs us even if we don't know why. In fact, the don't-know-why is always there. Koans work in that way too, with their particular kind of tantalising fascination. I was once taken, rather reluctantly, to see the ballet Swan Lake at the Royal Opera House in London. I am really not a high-art person and I was a bit out of my depth. Maybe being out of my depth was part of it. When I got there, I was so overwhelmed by the wordless beauty of the dance that I sat in the dark with tears rolling down my cheeks. How can we explain such moments? And do we need to? Too much explanation is a kind of force-feeding; it only leads to indigestion. It closes down the space where the reader could be making the jump themselves. So I truly hope you don't get indigestion or suffocate here. If you do, put the book down and sing to your cat.

A NON-SELF
SELF-HELP
BOOK

In a sense, this book is a snapshot of my life five years after my first book, *Stoep Zen*. Some of the same characters appear – my wife Margie, my daughters, a few old friends and relatives; the adults a little more stooped and more like children, the children a little less cute and more like adults. We still live on Poplar Grove, the small sheep farm near Colesberg in the dry Karoo. We still travel the dusty backroads far from the highway. We still meditate in the old shearing shed. Now and then I talk to friends from Lawyers for Human Rights who worked with me in the Karoo Law Clinic; we have all moved on to other things but we can look back over days when our lives were driven by a commitment to protect the weak and powerless. I still honour teachers and friends who daily inspire me; persons who live all over the world, persons from inside the Zen tradition and outside it. And, of course, I still give thanks for the voices I hear on the radio, which means we don't have television in the house yet.

There may also be some new words. Like 'Roshi', a respected teacher in the Japanese Zen culture. And 'koan', a teaching story, another word from Japanese Zen that has been absorbed into English. The words Dharma (the teachings) and Sangha (the community) are discussed in the text, as is Bodhisattva (a being of enlightenment). A zendo is a place of meditation. A bikkhu or a sannyasin is a monk, a homeless one. Ananda was the Buddha's attendant, Bodhidharma was the first patriarch of Ch'an (Zen) in China, Hui Neng the sixth. I have also drawn quotations and inspiration from two great Zen literary classics: the *Blue Cliff Record* and the *Book of Serenity.*

The Buddha is the person who inspired the Buddhist tradition; his name as a young boy was Siddhatta or Siddhartha, after he left home on his search for enlightenment he is often called Gotama (his family name), and he is sometimes referred to as Shakyamuni – the sage of the Shakya tribe. You will find my own version of the Buddha's life spread out through the book – the story of a boy whose mother died at birth, who grew up in privilege, whose conventional life could not fill the emptiness in his heart; the young man who left home to search for enlightenment when the suffering of the world became too painful for him to stay. Those of you who are familiar with the story of the woman who gave food to the Buddha-to-be before he attained enlightenment will see that I have avoided the traditional versions and made his muse a young farm girl.

THERE IS A BUDDHA
IN EVERY POTHOLE

Sometimes I talk about Zen practice. Practice is what Zen students
'do', the discipline they follow. The word holds in it a sense
of imperfection, of never quite getting it; it is also to do with
commitment, keeping at it whether we feel like it or not, whether
we are getting it or not; and it means implementing or embodying
something, as in putting a theory into practice.

Formally, the teachings of Zen are passed from teacher to student in
a continuing live transmission; in this way each teacher is an ancestor
in the tradition's lineage. For instance, I have received permission to
teach from Zen Master Dae Gak who received transmission from the
late Korean Zen Master Seung Sahn, and both Dae Gak and myself
have been students of the Japanese Zen Master Joshu Sasaki Roshi.

Then there are South African words here that may not be familiar to
everyone. A township sits alongside a town as the place where most
black people live; it's usually more destitute and more lively than the
town. A shebeen is a township tavern. I have used the term 'Bushman'
rather than 'Khoi-san' on good authority that it is once again the name
of choice. A dominee is a minister in the Afrikaans Dutch Reformed
Church, formerly the state church of the apartheid government. An

ayah is a nanny or nursemaid. Koeksuster and vetkoek are traditional Afrikaans delicacies. A braai is a barbeque. A bakkie is a small truck or utility vehicle. A koppie is a hill. A stoep is a stoop or verandah attached to a house. Boeremusiek is Afrikaans country music. Petrol is fuel or gas, the kind we put in cars. Oh yes, and a long-drop is an outhouse.

In *Stoep Zen* I looked at the open spaces of South Africa through a Zen lens. The open spaces are still there but the politics have changed – the heady days of the new democracy and the towering presence of Nelson Mandela have given way to the slow, painstaking building of a society that is still asking who it is and how to do whatever must be done. These are big questions, questions that need to be taken seriously, both privately and publically. Questions that need to be asked everywhere by everyone, not just in South Africa – it's just that in South Africa the questions feel so urgent, so raw. And, from the Zen point of view, the question remains of how we live whatever life the universe has thrown at us.

PREFACE

There is a song on the wind we can't quite catch. To hear it we have to stop. We have to set ourselves aside. And listen.

Under the hum of tyres and computers, beyond the relentless din of right and wrong, there lies a silence that holds the heartache and the longing of the world. And then, still further out, an empty road where wind and dust have wiped out all our tracks.

In this openness our hearts are lit. It is here that the singing starts. And our connection to each other and to the land will flow as naturally as the waters of the great Gariep that run under the bridge to the sea. We can find again this precious world in all its myriad forms. The sound of buses taking children off to school. An eagle-owl calling in the night. The cry of living in difficult times. And each becomes a doorway to the light.

I am not talking here of yet another way to put things right. I am talking about giving ourselves to this life completely, however it turns out. I am talking about selflessness. And that slippery, necessary word, love.

It is time to go home.

The party is over

Listen

One clear song turns the raft around

PART I
THE GREAT WAY

A monk asked Chau Chou, 'What is the Path?'
Chou said, 'It's outside the monastery gate.'
'I'm not asking about that path,' pursued the
monk, 'I'm asking about the Tao, the Great
Way.' 'Ah that,' said the Zen Master, 'For that
you take the N12 south of Kimberley, through
the back roads to Koffiefontein, Fauresmith,
Philippolis and Colesberg, then turn off the N9
onto the Oorlogspoort road.'

– ADAPTED FROM *BLUE CLIFF RECORD*, CASE 52

OUTSIDE OF KIMBERLEY I PULL IN AT THE FILLING STATION AND ROLL DOWN the window. A wave of heat floods the inside of the car. Nothing moves. A yellow flag stirs helplessly. I wonder if they've closed for lunch and whether I'll have to serve myself. Then, from under a pepper tree near the diesel pump runs a young man with flashing white teeth. I ask him to fill the car and clean the windscreen. We speak about the weather and about the rich people's 4x4s travelling down to the sea for the holidays. His skin is beautiful and very black, glinting in the sun like coal. When I say I am going home he says he already knows that because he can see it in my eyes. I tell him my home is hundreds of kilometres to the south, past Fauresmith, over the Orange river and into the far Karoo.

'That dry place,' he says.

'Yes. Dry and quiet. And tonight I'm going to sit on the stoep with my wife and a glass of whiskey and watch the sun go down.'

He looks at me with those great shining eyes, 'Like church,' he says. 'But without the choir.' Laughs at his joke. Then he looks around to make sure he isn't going to get into trouble for talking too long to a customer, even though there is nobody else in sight. 'Tomorrow I'm going to pay auntie Adams the last money for the dress.' It is the down payment on his little sister's outfit for her matric dance; tomorrow morning he will take his bicycle and his week's wages and ride down to the dress-maker to hand over the money. Then he will attend the graduation with the rest of his family, though he still needs black trousers to match his jacket.

I remember the day I gave the end-of-year speech at the local township school when the school leavers were presented in their formal clothes. How the families danced and sang in the hall as the young boys and girls walked up the aisle in their new suits and dresses to stand on the stage and face the people who had earned, borrowed, begged and sacrificed year after year so that these children could go all the way through school and graduate. And not to graduate casually, insultingly, as if it was nothing; it was a moment of intense pride and joy. I remember how, when everyone had taken their seats and the singing had died down, I was so overcome with emotion I couldn't speak. I asked for a glass of water. Eventually I just told them what was in my heart – that they had given me a great gift and that I hoped they would be able to go through their lives with the same gratitude and pride they showed that day.

I open my suitcase in the boot and pull out a pair of black legal trousers. The young man takes them and tells me to wait. 'Do not move,' he orders me. Then he runs off behind the building while I stand obediently at the car. The sun drills down relentlessly. Out he comes again in my work trousers and a black jacket, out to the thorn tree with its sparse leaves, where he takes up a position in the shade, legs apart, chest forward. And there he begins to sing. He sings an aria that I recognise, in a high tenor voice that is rich and clear. *Caro mio ben, credimi almen, senza di te languisce il cor* – Oh dearly beloved, believe me, without you my heart is filled with sorrow.

I am stunned. For there we are, the two of us – he under the thorn tree with his passionate vibrato soaring into the blue, me sinking down against the petrol pump, overcome with sadness and beauty.

That is the thing about South Africa. Despite all the separation, despite all the pain and mistrust and fear, we are still able to meet. Human to human. Openly and joyously. This is not something that only happens here but it is all the more astonishing here because of the separate lives we lead. So the intimacy is received with a gratitude that may look out of all proportion to the ordinariness of the interaction – a greeting on the street, a joke at the parking lot, dancing at a jazz festival. Of course these are small moments in a long life. And much must still be done to make society fair and efficient. But these small moments of connection are not to be pushed aside. In a fundamental way, they are deeply spiritual. Moments of awakening – like those in a bookshop when reading words that speak to us. Moments when our distractions drift to the background and we are left standing in a wider, more forgiving life. Moments in which we find the innocence and intimacy we so often long for, when the debate about Eurocentric culture in Africa is answered by a black man singing an Italian aria under a thorn tree. We all have experiences like this and it is important to remember them.

Sometimes we say the word Zen means meditation. Maybe a better word is awareness. Zen means being aware. Being awake. Being aware is the most natural thing in the world. You know you are sitting on a chair (or standing on your feet), you feel the pressure on your buttocks (or on the soles of your feet), the weight of the book in your hands, the touch of the paper, the itch on your nose. It is not difficult. You know when the car is on the road. You don't have to learn how to do it. You already know.

But we have a lifetime of distractedness to deal with, a habit of not paying attention which seems to block this natural awareness. So we undertake a discipline. This discipline is called meditation. Its job is to loosen the habits of inattention so that natural awareness can flow like a river.

I love the empty road. My eyes attend to everything but don't get caught anywhere. They see without trying. I welcome whatever comes into my field of vision, I let it all pass behind me without regret. From time to time an object claims me – a buzzard, a fence post, a springbok – then I let it drift back into its surroundings. In the Zen tradition this is called Shikantaza meditation – just sitting. Just driving. Just driving and seeing. Just driving and seeing and thinking. Letting the landscape flow through me as I flow through it. A mongoose runs over the tar to her burrow on the far side of the road.

The late Godwin Samararatne was a Sri Lankan meditation teacher who ran a meditation centre on a hill at Nilambe outside Kandy. To look at him, at such a loose transparent presence, you'd think you could blow him over. Up close, his reticence was endless. He made no dent in you at all so you had to lean in to him and that was when he would lift his head and smile right through you with a gentleness that was as strong and as pure as silk. Godwin visited South Africa a number of times to teach his beautifully plain form of meditation that owed as much to Krishnamurti as to the Buddha. At the time I met him I was still in my Japanese Zen monk's robes and we used to joke about him being a black man in white robes while I was a white man in black robes – I, of course, was in every way his junior yet his generosity was such that he always deferred to me.

Once Godwin stayed overnight with Margie and me at the farm, his only baggage a toothbrush in one pocket and some obscure oriental undergarment in the other. I think he was on his way to conduct a meditation weekend near Johannesburg. The next morning Margie drove him to the airport to catch a plane but she got lost and he missed his flight. Margie was mortified but Godwin just laughed – only western people get mad when things go wrong, he said; in Sri Lanka things go wrong all the time so we don't suffer so much. The two of them sat in the airport restaurant until the next connection to Johannesburg, Margie drinking tea, Godwin – as he often did – with his arms folded across his chest and his eyes shut, the faintest of smile in the corners of his mouth.

Zen Master Dae Gak lives on Furnace Mountain in eastern Kentucky. Although it is set in the spectacular Appellachian mountains, Furnace Mountain is just like Poplar Grove in being a place of dedicated Zen practice in a remote and conservative part of the country. I was fascinated to be there, in a place where old men wear dungarees and sit on stoops, where derelict back yards are filled with angry dogs and old cars, where cigarettes are not unfashionable and country music blares from every window. It was like stepping into a Norman Rockwell painting. And Dae Gak is one of the best-kept Zen secrets in the United States; he stays in a wooden hut with an outhouse far from the celebrity circuit, working part-time to support himself and living entirely for his students.

To my delight, Zen Master Dae Gak invited Margie and me to do a month-long retreat with him at Furnace Mountain; his wife Daniela was given a copy of *Stoep Zen* for her birthday and wanted to say hello. Writing is such a solitary occupation and it always makes me dance to hear that the book has touched someone. So we landed in Kentucky in deep winter and were welcomed like old friends. Margie and I at last had the chance to do a retreat together as guests instead of hosts, to sit alongside new friends in the beautiful Korean-style meditation hall. We threw ourselves into it with every bone in our body, grateful at each breath for the opportunity we had been given.

Meeting again they laugh and laugh
The open veld
The poplar grove

In South Africa we speak of Ubuntu – humanness or humanity. The word has been used so much since the advent of democracy that it has become a cliché; it is even used as a weapon by white people who accuse blacks of forgetting their Ubuntu when they are late for meetings. But if we can let those objections go for a moment, we can find again the true potency of Ubuntu. Umntu Ngumtu Ngabantu – a person is a person through other people. How wonderful! We are always in relationships, whether to another person or to a tree, a road, a steering wheel. If we are able to be truly present in that relationship then we attain Ubuntu. Then we are fully human. And at the same time we are connected to everything and everyone everywhere, like the old Indian image of Indra's necklace – a garland of jewels where each jewel reflects every other jewel and so contains the whole universe. In isiXhosa, when asked how I am, I reply in the plural; 'Siyaphila enkosi' – 'We are fine thank you'.

The Zen teaching of interconnectedness or interdependence says the same thing – in the last resort, there is only one thing happening here. We are all part of this singular pulsating interpenetrating organic life; Zen practice is to go beyond the idea of this and to embody it. Willing to be turned upside down and right-side up, willing for our hearts to be broken by the poignant beauty of our world. Then we will take care of each other and our children and our waterways as naturally as breathing in after a good sneeze.

A group of schoolchildren are walking along the side of the road in single file, some of them with their shoes in their hand. As I pass, each one of them lifts their arm to wave and then gets back to the long path home. Not complicated at all.

A student asks the Zen Master, 'What about an easy way home?' The Zen Master replies, 'That's like a pothole in the road. How will you avoid falling into it?'

In our yearning for peace and re-assurance we fill our lives with distraction – with family, with work, with the *Bold and the Beautiful*, with the state of the nation and the condition of the roads, with New-Age solutions and our spiritual progress. We look for short-cuts but they take us deeper into the veld. We head for Colesberg but the road goes to Cairo. Potholes are everywhere. There is no escape. We are lost. Lost? Wonderful! If we can be truly lost we are already home. Where else is there to go?

The sun on my right now
Falling across my lap
Whatever the politicians do or say
They can't take this away from me

'White man in Africa,' my friend Thandi tells me one day, 'You need
to find your ancestors or you will be lost forever.' Such a drama queen!
Not that she doesn't have a point, of course – English at home, Xhosa
on the street, Good King Wenceslas in summer, Buddha's birthday
in the fall, church schools and Buddhist monasteries. No wonder
things get a little mixed up sometimes. But you've also got to love it,
really, this upside-down life. So what if black men sing high opera in
Italian? So what if whites spend all their money on suncream – or if
Catholic Zen students pray to Mary Mother of God when their plane
hits turbulence over the Atlantic? Who decided life must be sensible?
Ancestry isn't about the contradictions of post-colonial society or the
colour of my great grandparents – though maybe that is part of it –
it's about living whatever life we are given, whichever way up it is.
It's about loving my life. When I do that, who isn't my ancestor?
I decide to scold Thandi for giving me a problem that isn't a problem
but she will only laugh. She is one of my ancestors; happily for me,
a living one.

The road straightens between a row of poplar trees
Leaves on my left
Leaves on my right
Tar straight ahead

There is a small café near the Riet river. Not really a café, just a house with a Coca-Cola sign on the front stoep, where Tannie Betsy makes old-fashioned food – she calls herself tannie (aunty) even though she is much younger than me. I don't think she makes any money out of her enterprise and she always treats me like the friend she has been waiting for all her life. This may be true for I never see anybody else there. As she fusses around me, cutting bread and brewing coffee, she talks without stopping. She tells me about her childhood home, how she grew up with the scent of baking, the smells of bread and rusks and tarts and the singing of her mother and the baking women. Betsy is moved by her own memories and her eyes brim with the telling of them. The sandwich is neatly wrapped, two hard-boiled eggs sit alongside it with neat twists of paper for salt and pepper and my thermos flask is tightly closed. She places all the food into an old-fashioned picnic basket, then she straightens up, takes my hands in hers and blesses me for coming all that way to stop at her house. I bless her back and walk out to the old Jeep, wondering when I will be able to give back the basket. She stands at her door and watches me until I am out of sight.

On our return from the Zen retreat in Kentucky, Margie and I were unable to sleep at night and we soon ran out of coffee. So off we went to town for supplies and there we met up with Long Bobby in the farmers' co-op, standing on his own with his walking stick in the corner of the store. We knew Long Bobby well; he isn't strong enough to work, he still lives at home with his elderly mother and all day long he walks the main street looking for someone to talk to. He is also very tall. With all her fierce sympathy, Margie went straight up to Long Bobby, ignoring the farmers leaning on the counter. Long Bobby told Margie his mother had just come out of hospital and she put her hand on his arm. I paid for our fencing wire and dog biscuits. We headed off to the café for groceries – especially coffee. Then Margie saw a basket of fruit which she bought for Long Bobby's mother and we drove off to his house under the koppie, a wonderful old place with a dovecote at the bottom end of town, smelling of ancestors and linoleum. There we found Long Bobby's mother sitting in her iron bedstead holding her night-dress to her throat. She thanked us for the visit and the fruit, we spoke about her illness and the kindness of doctors and we wished her a peaceful night.

Margie and I walked out onto the stoep with Long Bobby. He stopped and asked if he could pray so the three of us stood outside the front door holding hands while he called the blessings of Jesus Christ down upon us.

I fill my boat with moonlight
And row home

Death is in your face on a farm. Young lambs caught by a paralytic tick in the mountains lose the use of their legs and starve. A pair of bat-eared foxes lie side by side on the road after being flattened by a truck. A bird flies into a window. Flies fill the spider web outside the kitchen door. And a moth lies embalmed in the wax of a candle in the zendo. Sometimes it is difficult to look on this relentless extinction. But that is the truth about life; it dies. So Margie loads the dying lambs onto the back of the bakkie and takes them to the squatter camp where the children clap their hands and dance. Crows lift the foxes to their nest to feed the babies, the spider lays her eggs in the middle of her web and the cat pries loose the moth and swallows it.

Death is how life works. No death, no life. It is easy to miss this in the city but it is still there. Humans, kittens, bacteria, mosquitoes, cultures, languages, solar systems, digestions, loves, opinions, reputations – each one of them is only passing through. When we bow to this we can go beyond life and death; beyond our fear of death, beyond our clinging to life. We look it all in the face and respond with compassion. A road gets old and there are potholes. How will we look after it?

Today I walk
Slower
To the Post office

The Buddha Shakyamuni is the first ancestor in the Buddhist tradition, the first of Buddhism's Three Jewels. Whoever we imagine him to be or whatever we imagine him to represent, it is to him that we bow. The word 'Buddha' is an honorific title meaning the one who has seen. Maybe it is more helpful to look at his function rather than at his person. In this way Buddha is a process, the process of clarity functioning in the world. Like any process, it comes and goes. Sometimes we see clearly, sometimes we don't. Above all, it is not a solid fixed thing; it is not an idol. It is light in a field of light.

We also talk of Bodhisattvas in the Buddhist tradition. A Bodhisattva is a person whose life's work is to attain enlightenment together with all beings. He or she does not value liberation for themselves alone. Solitary enlightenment is meaningless anyway for, if we go deep enough, the usual sense of you and me as separate beings simply disappears. When we truly see, the self who sees and the tree that is seen are not the same little self and the same little tree they were before – now it's more like self-tree or tree-self. TreeandSkyandMe. Like the Buddha, the Bodhisattva is not so much a person as a function, the functioning of selflessness – sometimes here, sometimes not, sometimes this way, sometimes that. The Zen way is the Bodhisattva way. At the level of Zen practice we vow each day to free all beings, however many they are. At the level of attainment, there is no separation between ourselves and all beings; in this way, every moment of clarity is shared with the whole world. YouandMe! YouandMeandUs!

Sasaki Roshi used to talk about the absolute world and the relative world. The relative world is the world of greed, anger and delusion, the world of dissatisfaction, the world of Zen practice and the yearning for enlightenment. The absolute world is the place where everything dissolves in what he called the centre of gravity – BOOM! I was a monk with Sasaki Roshi but feel ashamed that I made so little use of my opportunity. I felt like a bird beating itself against the glass of Roshi's window. Maybe the problem was that I didn't beat myself to death. Since then I have had to take this disappointment in myself and plant it along the avenue of my life. At the time of writing this, Roshi is 105 years old and he is still giving interviews to his students. Everyone knows he will teach the Dharma until his very last breath – one of our great Zen ancestors.

Ten thousand houses
Knock at any door
Someone will answer

On the side of the road walks an elderly woman in a long coat. She reminds me of my friend Norman's mother, Ouma Jas, who was called Jas (the Afrikaans word for a coat) because nobody ever saw her without one. Ouma Jas is one of my revered ancestors. She was a formidable widow who was president of the local Christian Women's Temperance Union and a tireless campaigner against alcohol. Every day she would put on her coat and walk with her handbag down the backstreets of Colesberg to speak to Jesus in the Methodist church, to protest outside the shebeens and bottle stores and to visit the elderly.

Ouma Jas lived in a tiny two-roomed house stuffed with books and sheet music. When our daughters were small she used to leave a brown paper parcel on her stoep for them every birthday. That evening we would unwrap the parcel slowly and take out the books as if they were gold, reading them one by one around the fire on winter evenings.

One morning Margie and three other women sat around the kitchen table planning the first retreat for abused and orphaned children. The others were all dedicated church women, one of them a dominee. Margie took them on a tour of the rooms. When they reached the zendo she was anxious about the Buddha-figure on the altarpiece in case they were too uncomfortable to go in. She assured them it was not a golden calf. They all walked in anyway and the dominee said quietly, 'What a beautiful room. How present God is here.' That was when we knew the children's retreats would work, that these women would not allow anything to stand between them and their great work of love.

Our friend Nehli knits jerseys for the broken children at Margie's retreat. She wraps them in brown paper and sends them to Colesberg by post. At night the children kneel at their beds and thank her in their prayers. Nehli is 90 this year. Another ancestor.

Once a month I still put on my tie and suit to listen to workplace disputes. I love the work and my younger colleagues are interesting, respectful men and women who do their job with pride. Some days it feels as if the whole country is passing before me – lawyers in silk ties, white trade unionists, black shop stewards, unsophisticated farm workers. And all their suffering and beauty with them. One day a union representative entered an arbitration hearing in a grey suit with beautiful beaded braids in his hair. He bowed. 'Good afternoon,' he said, 'I am a national treasure.' And so he was. It didn't help him win his case though.

In the classical Buddhist tradition, qualities of the heart are called the four Divine Abodes. The four faces of love, four faces of enlightenment. Our work is to embody them in our lives. The first of the divine abodes is loving-kindness. Loving-kindness is our warmth toward all beings. Towards all of creation, in fact. It is grounded in our connection with all of life, in our sense of belonging in the place where we stand. From there our openness of heart flows quite naturally. Generosity is another name for it. And it is not a private warmth towards life in general (though it may be that too); it manifests itself concretely in each person or tree or sunset in front of us. Ah, nice to see you! How well you look today!

These qualities are more than just inner feelings. They are an expression of selflessness, a natural function of our world in the same way the sun is, or the moon. They do not come to us because we deserve them. And we cannot lose them, because they never belonged to us. During retreats, we end each day by sharing our practice with the world. We remind ourselves of our oneness with the world and vow to attain it. We own up to the loneliness and anxiety in our lives. We feel the pain of all people everywhere and take it into ourselves. We hold all beings in our arms. We say thank you for our great opportunity. May you be free from suffering. May you know joy. May you wake up.

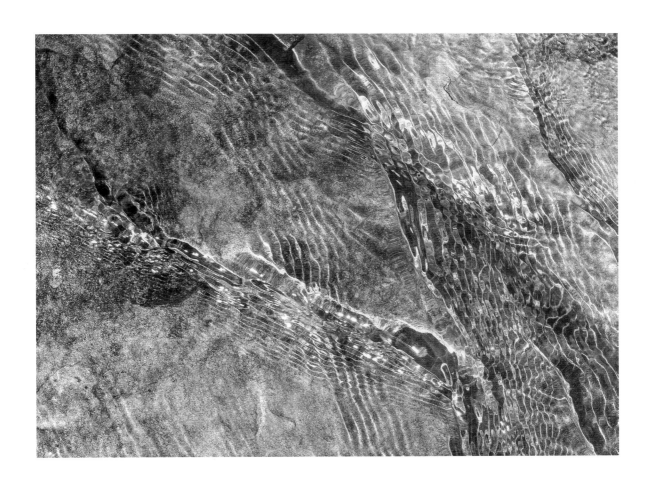

31

Just as I turn at the T-junction to Koffiefontein, someone is talking on the radio about Beyers Naude, the white Afrikaans dominee who repudiated the Dutch Reformed Church's teachings on the biblical basis of apartheid and moved with his family into a black community to take up the calling that defined his life. I heard Dominee Naude preach when I was a student. I don't remember what he said; I do remember being mesmerised and alarmed by the passionate shouts from the pulpit, so different from the measured comforts of our Anglican sermons. After the service, he told us why apartheid was a sin, how he had no choice but to say it and no choice but to live what he said. At all times he leaned forward in his chair, urgently needing to connect with each one of us. There was a point, also, when Naude addressed himself to the men from the security service standing in the back of the room in their shiny brown suits, 'And you from the police,' he said, 'You can tell your bosses what I am saying and maybe one night when they wake in fear of their children's future they will remember what you told them.' He was quite clever, we realised then, not just an innocent dove.

I also remember a television interview on Beyers Naude's 80th birthday, how he sat in an armchair, greeting his guests with old fashioned courtesy in his translucent pale skin. And I remember his friend Archbishop Tutu bouncing in like a mischievous boy. 'Oom Bey,' said Tutu, clapping his hands, 'I pray that when they come to write the history of this country they will write your name in letters of gold.'

These men are inspiring, unpretentious and genuine, radiating an unmistakable spirituality. They are my ancestors too. 'He has no sense of anyone being an Other to him,' someone is saying on the car radio about the archbishop. 'Desmond Tutu sees nobody as foreign or heathen – for him every person on this planet is part of his world and deserving of the same respect.' That is enough for me, I turn off the radio and drive on in the great silence.

Bikers are mad brave reckless people. I was never quite able to abandon myself to the lifestyle, even though I owned a number of motorbikes and professed to love it. It wasn't the spectre of my head rolling down the embankment that worried me, it was the thought of my knee grazing the tar. What I do remember is the instruction never to look at a pothole that I am trying to avoid. I was told to look beyond it at the road ahead because, if I tried too hard to miss the hole, I would drive right into it.

As a meditator I thought this was really interesting. Because meditation is the same. If we try to get rid of something in our mind, then the thing we don't like is going to hang around and bother us – a bit like trying not to think of a red donkey. All we can do is leave it free to graze in the field. It will move on when it is ready. Then we can open up to the next moment. And the next. At the side of the road I pass a yellow grader beside a corrugated iron shack.

I pull in under a pepper tree at the side of the road. I love pepper trees. It is an instinctive thing, I think – more than the delicate crescent leaves, more than the clusters of small red berries, more than the deep woven fissures in the cork-like bark; maybe it's a spiritual quality, one of outcast perseverance that is held 'upright with poise and grace' – to use the words of Zen Master Dae Gak. I sit at a small concrete picnic table under the tree and put my coffee flask and Tannie Betsie's picnic basket in front of me. This is how families used to eat when they travelled, I tell myself, eating food from their kitchens instead of takeaways, women wrapping hard boiled eggs in wax paper while men checked the oil levels in the car. So, in honour of all those ancestors on long journeys, I chew slowly on my eggs and sip mindfully on my coffee under the caress of the pepper tree. A ditch at the side of the road is full of water from a rain storm. A frog begins to call, letting me know I am accepted here in his world.

I think of travellers before cars. Of horsemen, of women with babies on their backs, of pilgrims, of walkers like Jesus and his disciples, of the Buddha in India five hundred years earlier who moved from place to place for forty-five years to teach. In the Buddhist tradition, the figure of Buddha is the corner stone; it is his enlightenment that inspired followers all over the world. But the story of the Buddha in classical literature is so mythic in its style that we can scarcely see the man behind it. Ironically for a teacher who refused to be treated as divine, the scriptures tell the story of a god, a story edited to make every step a cosmic event, resolutely removing all traces of his humanity. It may be my limited modern imagination that can't find the Buddha's belly in this epic but, instead of inspiring me, this saintly being seems to have had his teeth pulled and his ears flattened. I think of the time in the life of that young seeker after truth when all his yogic disciplines have left him defeated and ill, the hard nut of his ego more brittle than ever and his goal still out of sight, a time when he must have despaired deeply. So I sit there on the hard concrete bench with my indigestible cheese sandwich, wondering how lonely that must have been.

One small stone. Big enough to upend him, to tip him into the ditch at the side of the road. Big enough to tip him into Nothing. So he fell there without a murmur like a man asleep on his feet, unsurprised, unresisting, sliding into the mess of bugs leaves and skeletons of things long dead yet still there. So here we are Gotama, he told the tangle of his limbs, finally come to nothing in a small life, my glorious search for freedom ending in failure and defeat, with me not even caring if I live or die. Insects crawled into his navel then for here was a creature who could do them no harm and he let them be for he had come to the end, his body in ruins and the great peace calling him.

And as he lay there he slipped down the tunnel of his memory to the terraced lawns and the swept paths, to the little boy alone on the verandah of the great house, how still he stood there watching the families under the trees, the grownups laughing, the children running across the grass, the hawk love of the mothers. None of them seeing the small boy at the colonnade who watched their every move like a hungry dog, drinking in all that happiness until the servants came to call him for his dinner – Siddhatta the solitary boy in his thin skin of privilege.

The picture sank beneath his heart again, beneath his blackened skin and broken feet, his life slipping away into the foulness of the water, he giving himself up to things unbidden. From time to time there were feet along the road, feet that faltered at the sight of a man dying like a cow in a furrow and then hurrying on, leaving only the spiders in the dew-filled grass and the chittering of birds whose names he did not know. Gotama closed his eyes then. And waited. After all the years of beating down desire, he found himself awash with a strange new yearning, a yearning for release – alive and keen in his broken body.

He smelled again the bread baking in the kitchen – the kingdom of the women that was home to him, a place where he was never left alone, where he could stand beside his ayah watching the playfulness there while sunlight streamed through the window above the stove. Sometimes there were long deep pools of quiet when the bread was rising, the girls plaiting each others' hair, rubbing oil on each others' backs. And always his ayah in the corner opening peppers with those sharp nails, him next to her on his bare feet, grateful and safe.

One morning the ayah had called him to her stool, drawn him close and told him about his mother. How his heart had thudded in his chest! About the rich young beauty brought on a palanquin to marry his father, her delicate fingers and downcast eyes. How that summer her belly had swelled with the child inside her, her ankles sore, her breasts full, how when her time came the ayah and her helpers gathered round the bed, guards at the windows, astrologers at the door, how they drew out the slippery boy but when the yells of the mother grew weak then stopped, the lord his father walked out beyond the banyan trees from where he uttered a cry so terrible the children were brought inside, the servants hushed and the shutters closed. How after that the man never came to see his son, how the wet nurse was called from the village to suckle him, how they raised him in the kitchen – there where the ayah now spoke in her low voice – where the young girls sang to him and tickled him, where he laughed for them and ate his toes, where they threw him into the air and caught him until he grew big enough to wobble on the lawn on his little legs and how at last one afternoon his father came from his rooms to watch the boy, and the ayah and the servant girls saw him take the little hand and walk with him along the path in the slowness of love and they wept to see it.

So the tattered yogi dreamed his restless dreams, where even the longing for peace now lost its hold and his body found its place among the smallest and most detested creatures, his sleep the sleep of the lost.

Siddhatta had given himself to his boyhood then — in running races and climbing trees, in bows and arrows, monkeys and parrots, stories and stars, in the teasing of the girls in the kitchen, in his ayah's soft voice, and in tickling his friend Channa so the two of them lay laughing until they cried — and behind it all the hem of his father's robe, the sandaled foot beneath the perfect palms. But even then, in the stillness of the night while the world slept, Siddhatta felt the holes in the canopy through which the cold wind blew. Until one evening as he and his father met for prayers he dared to ask the question whose answer he so feared. 'Just tell me,' he whispered, 'Just tell me did she hold me before she died?' But as the lordly pock-marked face trembled and capsized a hand was already pulling him off his feet to the children's quarters and when he looked back his father was still staring to the west where it was growing dark, the long flat clouds tunnelling down through the ending of the day and him watching to see if the man would turn and see him but he didn't.

That night it rained again and the wet leaves softened against Gotama's body like a poultice, their scent lifting into the air. He wondered where his sannyasin's life had gone with its penance and its pranayama but he found only the dampness on his ruined skin, the stings the bites the scuttling legs, the whole world living and dying around him, him just lying there unnoticed like a small boy in a kitchen and untroubled in a nothing sort of way.

PART II

A NARROW BRIDGE

Let short things in your life be short. Let long things in your life be long. Stop cutting and patching everything. The follower of the Way has to drive slowly over the narrow Koffiefontein bridge.

– Adapted from the *Book of Serenity*, case 20

Nobody believed it could be done. But in 2010 South Africa hosted a wonderful Soccer World Cup. Gratefully, we relived the unity and optimism of our first democratic election. The stadiums were built on time, thieves put away their knives and turned on their televisions. And although our own team was knocked out early in the tournament, the people of this country danced and blew their vuvuzelas. At the farm I would walk up to the workers' house to watch the games on their television, discovering that soccer is at its best with chickens wandering under my feet.

On the field it was just as interesting. The Italians dropped out of the competition in a flood of tears and ran down the tunnel to the changing room. The French lost to South Africa and their coach refused to shake hands. The South Africans didn't make it into to the second round but after they lost they ran round the field celebrating. And when the Japanese were thrashed by Uruguay in the quarterfinal, they lined up in front of their supporters and bowed.

My car still has little South African flags on its side mirrors, not in support of the national team but in support of all the people who had faith in our generous welcome. If you are not attached to winning or losing then every game is a good game. Kick the ball. Kiss the coach. Give your opponents a handkerchief.

The day is hot so I wind down the window to feel the dry air on my face. Beyond a group of gum trees on my left I see a small church beside an empty farm house. To my astonishment I hear a bell ringing from the steeple as I pass by, a single bell tolling in the veld. I tell myself to stop and meet the person who is pulling on the bell rope but I drive on. A flood of memories assail me. I remember a Quaker meeting house in a remote village in Wales where I was greeted by a man who had been meditating there on his own for eleven years; 'I was just sitting here in case somebody came,' he said. 'And here you are!' I also remember being woken by the Sunday morning church bells in Chichester, England, where I taught Latin and Divinity to choirboys at the cathedral school; I used to lie in bed listening to bells falling in and out of time as they rang out over the fields, me in my pyjamas with my hands behind my head. At the top of the cathedral bell tower was the silent room, where the ringers stood on a circle of small red mats, leaping onto ropes that hung through the ceiling to pull them down, with only the creak of the ropes there and the faraway sound of the bells above. How long ago those memories. How they touch me still in this strange land.

Retreats are a good time to remember our ancestors. At Furnace Mountain the cabins are spread out among the trees. We get up long before dawn and walk to the meditation hall along narrow footpaths, black figures in a black night. As I walk, my forbears in this practice walk beside me, those countless generations in faraway mountains; women and men who, like us, put aside their dreams to pull on robes and head into the night, whether they feel like it or not. All around me are tall silent trees. I shine my torch on the snow in front, feeling Margie's soft step behind. In the corner of my eyes I see other torches flashing through the trees like fireflies, all of us going the same way. Towards the light.

I pass the place where my friend Johannes fell off his motorbike. Johannes is a middle-aged Afrikaner who used to be a minister in the Dutch Reformed Church before his lost his faith, his wife, his teeth, his dignity and all that was dear to him. He was left with only his wonderful teenage children.

That was when Johannes fell in love with a beautiful Indian girl from Steytlerville, not much older than his wonderful teenage children. He and this girl were different in all respects imaginable: she was a devout Christian, she ate her curry hot, her life lay ahead of her and she wanted at least seven children.

Despite these differences – or perhaps because of them – Johannes knew he was in love. But he wasn't sure how to approach the gulf between them. I told him, 'Listen, this is the new South Africa: learn to live with differences.' Johannes, poor man, believed it. He had to find out how she felt and so he organised a very long and roundabout road trip on his motorbike to visit her. On the way back he laughed and sang and talked to himself until the visor of his helmet fogged up. He opened the visor to smell the fields and the fuel and heat and the tar and he fell off between the Petrusburg junction and the Koffiefontein bridge. He has never told anyone what happened in Steytlerville.

People like to ask, 'But what did the Buddha teach?' Despite the voluminous scriptures of the tradition, according to the Buddha himself, his Dharma – his teaching – was very simple; 'I teach suffering and the end of suffering,' he said.

So let's start at the beginning, with suffering, even if it is difficult to think of it on an open road with the sun at my back. Suffering has two parts to it. The first is the doomed nature of the world we find ourselves in – a transient place in which everything is designed to grow old and die, including ourselves. The second part is our reaction to this uncontrollable and disappearing world; it can range from frustration, irritability and the deadly slow drip of depression, to an anguish so strong that we do not know how to survive it. All this is the unavoidable presence of suffering in our lives. Look it in the eye, says the Buddha; accept it, for this is the place to start.

We all respond to suffering in different ways. We turn to drink, we work late, we join a church that promises heaven. Or we take up Zen practice. We learn to meditate. Our minds slow down and our hearts begin to open. But sooner or later we uncover subtle layers of suffering there too. We find that what we call our spiritual path has become yet another strategy of the ego, a tactic to avoid one part of our life and grasp another, to escape suffering and find enlightenment. We remain divided.

Seeing this is wonderful. For, in truth, we are not dealing with freedom *from* suffering but freedom *in* suffering. When we truly accept this – even for a moment – we find ourselves living in the space beyond both suffering and the end of it. We have attained the teaching of the Buddha. Then suffering is just suffering and the end of suffering is just the end of suffering. That is it – just the Ouch! and the Aaah! of our one life.

There is another point about suffering but it will have to wait because a large truck is right behind me. I can see the huge chrome grille, two enormous headlamps and a bumper big enough to push me off the road. Time to drive more attentively.

There is a small farm stall near the road that serves English-style breakfast all day – dark stewed tea, eggs with greasy chips, baked beans. By now it is early afternoon. A huge white man and a small black man walk in with red overalls and tattooed arms. 'Cyril's Cylinders' it says on their backs. When the waitress comes out with a tray of hot food she stops dead. In front of her the two men are holding hands, their eyes tight shut as they pray. They finish and look up to her. She puts the tray on their table. The grace has changed the place as clearly as the sun shining through the window.

I stop and talk to a traffic cop leaning against his car near the old single-lane Koffiefontein bridge. We shake our heads at the heat and point to clouds gathering in the north. He tells me that the only thing growing on the far side of the bridge is potholes – potholes, nothing and still more nothing. 'But then sir,' he tells me, 'I suppose if you can't ride through a bit of bugger-all in this life you won't get to the bottle store on the other side.'

In Bloemfontein there is a music academy where township children learn classical music. For my sixtieth birthday I bought myself a double bass and joined one of the lesser string groups, the orchestra for nine year olds. I could never find my place on the sheet music but the children enjoyed helping me, happy to point out where I should be playing; 'Not there uncle – here!' At the academy they learn in the old-fashioned way under the guidance of teachers who give up every weekend to impart a love of playing. One morning a little boy was trying to explain the un-musical marks in his music book. He said there was no room at home to play his violin so he practiced in the long-drop below the vegetable patch. It was there, when he tried to turn a page, that one of the papers floated into the pit below and he had to call his brother to hold his feet so he could retrieve the lost score. The teacher pulled the boy to her and hugged him, ruffling his hair to disguise her emotion. I hear he now plays second violin in one of the country's professional orchestras.

The road is clear now. The big truck turned off at the silos and I can get back to my contemplation of suffering.

But I find that my thoughts about this, which promised to be so interesting, turned off at the silos with the truck and there is only a row of gum trees on my left, tall and dignified in the morning sun. Purple trees and a clear blue sky above. How I wish this for all people, whoever they are.

On the swift flowing river
Tossing a ball
When it lands in the water it sweeps away
Who can watch it?

I pass the Koffiefontein entrance with its oversize coffee pot. Water pours through the spout into a bucket below and children are splashing each other in their underwear. A dark unused mine dump looms over the town and men without work stand in the street; but I hear from the shopkeeper that they are re-sifting the old ore with new machinery and finding diamonds again. It was at Hopetown, near here, that the first diamond was found by the children of a farmer while they were playing in the dirt; the farmer thought the stone was pretty so he gave it to his neighbour as a gift. That was in 1866. Then the stone was bought from the neighbour by an English adventurer called O'Reilly who took it down to Grahamstown where it was officially identified as a diamond. O'Reilly passed through Colesberg on his way south and the men in the Empire hotel bar laughed at him when he told them he had a diamond in his pocket. So he took the stone and scratched his daughter's name on a window pane in a house in the main street. Over a hundred years later that house became the Karoo Law Clinic – where I had my human rights law office – and the pane of glass still had the name 'Adelaide' inscribed in copperplate script on the glass.

When there was a threat that white right-wingers would throw stones at the law clinic in the early 1990s, I took out the pane and gave it to the local museum who didn't really care about it so one day I walked in and took it out again under my arm. Now it hangs on a wall at the farm and I can tell the story to anyone who comes to visit. The elegant Victorian law clinic building, with its curved tin roof and filigreed ballustrade, is now a face-brick bottle store.

A running stream beside the old mountain path
Deep in the clouds the old temple bell

After her husband's death, Ouma Jas had sole use of the family car, an old grey Hudson Super-6, which was immediately put to use in her charitable works. It was also used to take the neighbourhood children to the river – little bodies piled on laps, along the back window and even in the boot with a plank of wood propping up the door for air.

But the Super-6 was not a good starter. Ouma Jas, always anxious to set off, would force the ignition, the pump would flood and the engine would turn until the battery started to run down. She would tell the children to sing a chorus so they'd sing, 'Trust in the Lord and don't despair'. After the third verse the car would splutter into life. 'Praise the Lord!' she would cry, grinding the car into gear. Some of the older boys may have wondered if Ouma Jas hadn't just given the sodden pump time to clear itself but, as she reversed out of the garage, Jas knew in her heart that the Lord, together with His creature the Hudson Super-6, tests our faith in mysterious ways.

I remember a Catholic nun who attended one of my retreats, how I tried to make the Zen tradition comfortable to her as a Christian. 'I don't want to feel comfortable,' she said, 'I want you to knock me to my knees.' The world isn't a sensible place and it doesn't help to make it one.

A group of people are standing around an old Nissan bakkie at the side of the road. When I stop, they tell me their back tyre is flat. I open my boot and take out my jack and together we get the Nissan into the air. The tyre must have been ridden flat for quite a distance, it smells burned and is completely useless. As the men put on the spare, I tell them about my mother and the first car she nearly saw. She was a young girl then and a horseman came to the farmhouse to tell them a four-wheeled machine would be driving up the road on its way to Colesberg. My mother and her sister combed out their hair and put on their church dresses but, by the time they got to the road, the car had already passed and all they could do was watch the cloud of dust in the distance. That was when my mother put her face to the ground to smell the tyre tracks. 'There is one thing I have never forgotten,' she told us, 'The smell of rubber tyres on gravel.' The men wind down the jack and put it back in my boot. We shake hands, all fifteen of us, and I get into my Jeep and drive on. My mother, my ancestor.

My friend Croft once spent a few months at Godwin Samararatne's meditation centre at Nilambe, a simple place with few facilities some distance from town. One afternoon an argument broke out among some of the European residents about a taxi driver who was meant to pick them up and take them shopping but didn't. They were standing around blaming the driver, blaming Sri Lanka, blaming their situation, when Godwin walked up with his umbrella under his arm and asked what the problem was. They told him how the taxi driver had let them down. 'Oh,' said Godwin. He opened his umbrella and began to walk down the hill to the town, a dark man in white robes under a bright yellow disc. After a while, they followed him.

Croft loved Godwin. He said one day Godwin was talking to some young Sri Lankan monks and he asked them what the most difficult thing was about their lives in the monastery. Meditation, they said. And what is the thing they most enjoyed, he asked. Playing with the dog, they said. So, said Godwin, why don't you meditate like you're playing with the dog?

The road settles around me. I let go of my thoughts. I run my mind through my body to relax – my neck, my shoulders, my stomach, my arms. Then I breathe out slowly and gather in the hills on each side of the road, a pothole which I swerve to pass, and light sparkling on a distant farmhouse roof.

Of course my father is also my ancestor. He was a school teacher for most of his life. I recently met a middle-aged man who told me that my father had been his housemaster when he was a small boy at boarding school. He told me how he used to cry at the beginning of term when his parents brought him back to the hostel. And he told me how, on that terrible first night, my father would always put a chocolate under his pillow.

It is time for a stop beside the thorn tree at the side of the road, time for a detour into history. The road I am travelling is old and filled with voices; we need to honour them. The tyres crunch on the gravel, I switch off the engine and silence sweeps into the car.

This is a region defined by dryness, by distance from the seats of power and by the great Orange river – sometimes called the Gariep – that runs westward through the arid plains until it reaches the Atlantic. I am not a historian. But I was fortunate enough to take part in land claims around here, where dispossessed communities were given a chance to recover their ancestral ground. That meant reading papers locked in trunks for generations, it meant raiding the shelves of archives, it meant listening under trees to tales told by old men and women. Much of what I heard was filled with sadness. And most of the dispossession remains un-remedied because it took place too long ago to qualify for restitution in the politics of today.

The first creatures in these great plains were the animals, the herds that came here to drink, to breed, to hunt. With them lived the Bushmen, in a harmonious but bloody rhythm of seasons, life and death. Then came the waves of in-comers from the Cape. Eccentric groups of all races were already moving into the interior during the eighteenth century, all of them eager to get away from a society that stifled them, spurned them or tried to hang them – runaway slaves, military deserters, common criminals, dreamers, hunters and missionaries. In the hinterland they fell under the protection of warlords along the Gariep, where small armies on horseback stole each other's cattle and women.

The next great wave was the migration of white Dutch boers, farmers who left after the English took over the Cape and especially after the abolition of slavery there in 1834. The boers trekked in extended families with great herds of stock, armed with guns and a biblical conviction of white superiority. Inevitably they met up with the people of the interior and, also inevitably, the boers ended up with the land while the locals were left with hangovers and empty treaties. Then they all had to cope with the arrival of the last wave – white fortune hunters in search of diamonds. There was just one thing the waves of visitors from the south had in common; they all hunted the animals and the Bushman. I am told the last permit for shooting Bushman was issued in 1936.

So this place is ancient. Its traces can be seen in fossilized trees and Bushman rock engravings, in the creased faces of the wandering cart people – the karretjiesmense – and in diamonds on well-shaped fingers; it is here in deserted mine dumps, in church steeples, quaint Victorian cottages and tin shacks, in blockhouses and concentration camps. Amid the cycles of stability, dispossession and renewal, people build and plough and watch the moon at night, they nurse babies, feed their children and close the eyes of the dead. They make love in wartime and they die in times of peace. The world is vast and wide, far beyond our control; the world is also concrete and precise, needing meticulous attention and care. So what are we to do? I cannot comprehend it at all. But when it is time to move on again, I look into my rear view mirror and pull out into the road.

We often associate a spiritual path with purity and decency. Of course that is what we would like for ourselves but we have to be careful because these goals – like any other ideas – can squeeze the juice out of our life. Politeness and orderliness, while helpful in a post office queue, are not enough. We need to reach higher than nice, wider than good and deeper than respectable. Think, rather, Jesus storming into the temple to turn over the tables of the money-changers or Zen Master Lin Chi shouting and whacking his students with a stick to wake them up. That kind of directness. Try diving head-over-heels into our very vulnerability and humanness, into the chaos of the rush hour traffic with its hooters, fumes and fists. What will we find there? We do not know. Dare we look? Whatever we find, it will be real.

The Great Way cannot be known
Open your mouth
Raindrops on your tongue

A young woman with a red flag waves me down at some road works. She has earphones in her ears and is jiving to unheard music. On the radio someone is talking about Eugene de Kock, the notorious former security policeman and head of a police death squad during the apartheid era. De Kock was called 'Prime Evil' for his brutal ways but he decided to co-operate with Lawyers for Human Rights when they broke the story of the hit squads, which the government had denied for years. He was charged for his many crimes and is now in prison for the rest of his life. At the Truth and Reconciliation Commission, De Kock told how he and his colleagues drank brandy and braaied meat over a fire while the corpse of an activist they had just assassinated was burning on the same flames. 'We had to get rid of the evidence,' he said.

But then the radio interview goes on to a story in the exercise yard of Pretoria Central prison, where De Kock found a new prisoner by the name of Stefaans Coetzee. Coetzee is a young white Afrikaner who confessed to bombing a group of black people in the town of Worcester. According to the voice on the radio, De Kock cornered Coetzee and told him to get rid of his racism. 'If you don't,' said De Kock, 'You will be in two prisons – one at Pretoria Central and the other in your heart.'

The woman with the flag lifts the barricade and lets me through. I wave at her. She waves back. What more do we want from this life?

Zen Master Dae Gak's Dharma talks at Furnace Mountain are wonderful. He always starts by clearing his throat and cleaning his glasses, umm-ing and aah-ing to settle himself. After that he reads a koan from the *Blue Cliff Record* – that spectacular poetic collection from twelfth century China. Long silences punctuate his words as he searches to connect with the text and his students. Then, as he reaches deeply into himself, I become aware of a resonance, like an overtone in music, ringing out above the words. Afterwards, I can never remember what he said but I respond in the only way I can – with tears. Then I hobble outside to stand alone among the poplars where each leaf is sharp and bright in the crisp morning sun.

My friend Chrisi turned 60 the other day. She lives in a smart house in Durban with her husband and two cats, Sky and Hemmingway. As I drive over the ding-ding of a railway crossing I try to remember what I wrote her on her birthday.

Dear Hemmingway and Sky

I must first commend you on your fine names and your smooth coats.
Of course I am flattering you but I need a favour.
I am asking for your help with the woman of the house.
You may think she is beyond redemption but that is not the point,
You have to try try try for eight full lives
Otherwise you will come back as tinned fish.

You have stumbled upon a cat's paradise but even in heaven there is suffering
So this practice of selfless mischief is very necessary for you
If you want to become great Zen Clowns.
Now is the time to show the feline steel under those glossy robes
To manifest it in the human world.

You can begin by turning upside down the way she looks at things –
Remind her that she has made her husband, my Dharma brother, a happy man
Remind her that curtains need to be a little ripped and sofas to have threads hanging
out of them
That wrinkles are the lines of life
That flying through the air is not undignified
That she is beautiful beyond her two long legs
And a good friend.

By hiding in the cupboard you will teach her loss
By tumbling down the stairs you will teach her laughter
By getting under her feet you will teach her patience
And by lying on her lap you will bring her joy.

You will only know that you have succeeded in your work
When she doesn't tidy up
When she turns somersaults on the carpet
When you hear her throwing pillows at the old man
And purring as she curls up beside him.

The day she realises that all this wonder is under her elegant nose
She will become the cat you know she can be.
Only then will your great work be done.
In the meantime, smooth down your whiskers and sing
Happy Birthday, Dear Chrisi, Happy Birthday to You!'

Rain must have fallen here last night. The potholes are filled with water. And when the sun comes out from behind the clouds it shines in puddles all over the road.

Between Erfdeel and Fauresmith men are digging a ditch. A white man in a hat and short pants poses like a statue with one foot on a rock, arms folded over his enormous stomach. Beside him, black men in red overalls raise their picks in unison. I lift my hand in greeting as I drive past. The white man doesn't move. The black men all put down their tools and wave.

Dharma, as we saw, is the name given to the teachings of Buddhism. But the Dharma doesn't mean only official Buddhist teachings. It means The Truth. As Buddhists have never claimed sole access to The Truth, this can be any religious, spiritual or secular teaching that speaks to the heart. I still have a little card sent out to friends and family on my grandparents' fiftieth wedding anniversary where they quote the beautiful prayer of Alcoholics Anonymous – Lord grant me the serenity to accept that which I cannot change, the courage to change what I can, and the wisdom to know the difference. Pure Dharma. More ancestors.

Cold moon
High wind
On the ancient cliff
A twisted apricot

Each season at home a small group of thin-legged boys and girls climb out of a truck and stand close together in front of the house. They are welcomed by women with wide arms who listen to their stories in the zendo and let them swing from trees in the poplar grove. By Sunday afternoon these fragile little beings are running around like real children again. There are neighbours who say, 'But what's the point, a weekend won't change their lives!' Of course. A weekend doesn't take away the ten thousand difficulties the children will face. But the ten thousand difficulties also don't take away this – that they can look back and remember a moment in an old farmhouse in the veld where they received more love than they ever knew was possible in this world. And felt completely, totally safe.

Little Themba is nine. Last year his father and his mother were killed in a road accident. He was their only child and now he stays with an aunt who doesn't want him. Since the accident Themba stopped talking, he stopped playing with friends and he stopped singing the hymns at morning assembly. His teacher called Themba in one day and gave him a shoe box. She told him to go home, to find things that remind him of his parents and to keep them in the box. The next day he came and showed his teacher what he had brought – a sock and a packet of matches that belonged to his father, a feather his mother used to put in her hair, a cup she used to drink from. Now Themba sings at assembly and talks a little in class. And during break time he sits by himself under the pepper tree in the playground looking at all the precious things in his shoebox.

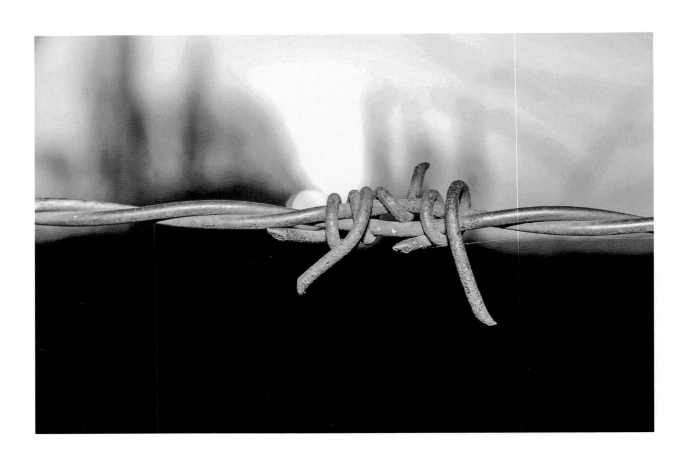

78

Under a stand of gum trees a small boy runs around the side of a house, a man behind him. I can't tell if they are playing or not.

I remember the court photographs in my first High Court trial as an advocate. I was appointed to defend a man by the name of De Jager who was accused of murdering his family. He had also tried to shoot himself but that had failed. When I met Mr De Jager in the cells beneath the court he refused to look at me. I began paging through the prosecution's photos and saw his wife with her head blown off in a kitchen chair, I saw his two little boys crumpled on top of each other in front of the fridge as they tried to get away. I closed the album. We sat there without a word, my heart thumping in my ears. Then De Jager said softly, 'I just want to die.' Those were the days of the death penalty and my job was to get my client off on the charges and out of the noose; he wanted to plead guilty and be hanged. My nightmare had come.

Eventually, I let Mr De Jager tell his own story and left it for the court to decide what to do. All De Jager said in the witness box was, 'My Lord, I beg you, do not let me live.' The judge found him guilty on three counts of murder but he was a new judge who was determined not to impose the sentence of death in his first case. So he found, quite reasonably, that the accused had been demeaned by his wife and all the empty brandy bottles to the point of desperation and gave him twenty years in jail. When I went to visit Mr De Jager in prison to see how he was getting on, the warders told me he had hanged himself in his cell that morning. It is a story of terrible suffering from every angle, but what I cannot forget is the two small boys whose last memory on this earth was of their father hunting them down with a shotgun.

Gus the sheepdog is not caught in words. He is too clever. When I trained him I taught him the conventional instructions – 'Come By' around to the left, 'Away' around to the right. Then I handed him over to Tongo Januarie, the stockman. Tongo got the instructions the wrong way round – 'Come By' to the right, 'Away' to the left. But the dog was never fooled. He went wherever he needed to go to bring in the sheep.

What is the meaning of this life? Go ask your dog.

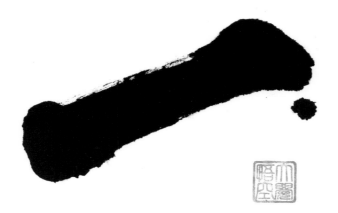

Jesus in the coffee grinder
Buddha in the sink
Bodhidharma in the corner
With his noonday drink.

We sink into our cushions
And our life begins to flow
Stomachs sigh and grumble
Desires come and go.

I should not have gone to China
Voted left instead of right
But when I let my breath out
It's airy and it's light.

Around me markets tumble
The cupboard shelves are bare
But we still have the sky above
And breathe its tender air
Its tender air.

We have ancestors in all facets of our life. My writing ancestor was a man by the name of John Saunders. John was an enthusiastic young teacher at my junior school who helped me through a difficult time to retrieve my enthusiasm for life. He now lives in Oxford as a retired academic and after *Stoep Zen* was published I received an affectionate letter from him, telling me that he still had an old school magazine in which I wrote the story of Noah landing his ark in the dry Karoo.

Last year John and his wife came out to South Africa to escape the English winter and were travelling down to Cape Town by South Africa's premier luxury train, the Blue Train. I drove to Kimberley station and stood on the platform with a bunch of carnations and a bottle of wine. Premier does not mean punctual and I had four more hours to wait in the midday heat, walking up and down the platforms under the Victorian lamps. Then all of a sudden there was a ringing of bells and men in black uniforms made their way onto platform one, buttoning their jackets and polishing their shoes on the back of their socks. The white man from the railway museum rolled out a red carpet, muttering about the holes in it since the blacks took over. Then the train pulled in with the men in their uniforms standing to attention and the wealthy visitors streamed out into the heat.

By now I was quite nervous and suddenly there was John Saunders
in front of me, as gentle and as recognisable as he was fifty years ago.
How deeply happy it made me to see him, as if some cellular memory
had broken the surface. I handed his wife the flowers and him the
wine and we sat in the dining car to drink expensive whiskey served
by old fashioned waiters. I talked too anxiously and too fast, they
listened attentively and patiently and then the whistle blew and I was
hurried back onto the platform. With a waving of flags the train glided
out, John Saunders already asleep in a chair by the window of his
compartment as it picked up speed, oblivious to my heartfelt waving.
Maybe it was the afternoon whiskey or maybe, I rather hoped, the
meeting was as exhaustingly beautiful for him as it was for me.

My mind is like the autumn moon
Clear and bright in a pool of jade

Zen Master Su Bong was a friend of Zen Master Dae Gak and used to visit him on Furnace Mountain. There was an argument one day about trees that had been cut down to make way for the new temple. Some people were furious that the precious trees had been killed. Others were furious that trees could be more important than the new building. Everyone had a strong opinion. Su Bong stood at the edge of the clearing looking over the valley below. 'Beautiful view,' he said.

It always wakes us up when someone can keep a wider perspective, one that is not stuck in right and wrong. In the early days of the law clinic in Colesberg, Margie and I made friends with a retired couple in town. They were rather eccentric; Hubert wore an eye patch from the war, which nobody believed, and Esther played solitaire in bed. They sold the law clinic building to me for a pittance when the businessmen in town tried to keep us out. We knew that Hubert and Esther had health problems and that they were depressed at the prospect of becoming older, sicker and poorer. One Friday in winter I got a phone call from Hubert asking me how I was; 'I was just wondering,' he said. Sunday morning we had another call. It was from the neighbour who told us that Hubert and Esther had locked themselves in their garage, started the car and died of carbon monoxide poisoning while holding each other's hand.

The whole town had an opinion on the tragedy – some said it was a sin, others that it was cowardly. When Zen Master Su Bong heard about it he said only, 'How they must have loved each other!'

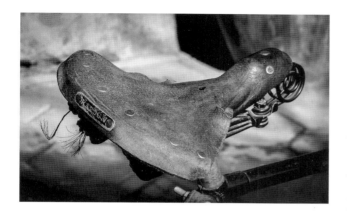

Near a turn-off to a place without a signboard there is a collection of small houses. I presume they are for farm workers until I see a brightly painted tin wall with pictures of dagga (cannabis) plants around the windows and graffiti about Lord Jah on top of the door. Rastafarians and farms don't usually go together. But maybe the new South Africa has more surprises than we know.

Of course it sparks another memory, one about an academic presentation at the university in Bloemfontein. Conferences about the new South Africa are endless; their redeeming feature is usually the morning tea break, when participants can gather cheerfully for coffee and cakes, where the intimacy of food and light-hearted banter turn out to be more healing than the speeches. One day I was giving a far-too-earnest paper on inter-faith reconciliation when there was a disruption at the back of the hall. All the middle-aged white men in suits and all the middle-aged black men in suits turned in irritation. Who could be so disrespectful? And in walked the Rastafarians, the bishop at the front, a parade of attendants behind him – distinguished black men in tall purple hats, long beards, royal blue robes and wide smiles. Inter-faith dialogue at its clearest!

Meditation. It is what we do to recover our natural wakefulness. And to do this we need a more spacious kind of attention, an awareness of what is happening in our mind rather than being stuck in the content of it. But this attention has to be feather-light; just a touch of recognition and then we let it all go – pfff! So, instead of just believing what we think, we see that we are thinking. Instead of just longing for a dog, we see the longing. Thoughts and dogs come and go, thinking and wanting come and go. Like clouds.

Already our life is less obsessive. Already we recover a sense of humour. We are no longer dragged around by our thoughts, by our desires or our fears, and there is blue sky everywhere. Then we let go of meditation altogether and rest in the wonderful natural functioning that sticks nowhere. Thinking is just thinking. Wanting is just wanting. And the dog is just the dog again, with her black coat and wagging tail.

The second Divine Abode is Compassion. Sympathetic sorrow – the spontaneous opening of our heart at the suffering of another. It is the heartache of the world coursing in my blood. It is hearing the cries that come to us on the wind and up the street, from bedrooms, boardrooms and classrooms. Compassion cannot be learned, it is simply the natural functioning of a heart that is clear and open. And because it is selfless, it can be as soft as a duckling or as fierce as a tiger. Light as a leaf in the wind.

There is a famous photograph of Archbishop Tutu when he was presiding over the hearings of the Truth and Reconciliation commission. After all these years I can still hardly look at it. It shows him at a hearing in East London when a mother was talking about her son who was picked up by the security police, how she had waited all those years with a broken heart for the boy who never returned. In front of the audience and the world's television cameras, the archbishop put his head down on the desk and wept.

Thandi is right. I have to find my ancestors. But I haven't lost them because I am a white man in Africa (or an African in America or a Tibetan in India). I lose them when my direction is not clear. When I can drop my life of self-concern, angels and ancestors line my path and bodhisattvas sing in the apricot tree. In such a world Thandi's challenge disappears, for here no-one is a stranger. Not even me.

Near Fauresmith two young horses race each other along the roadside fence. They play with me –catching up, dropping back, catching up again. I can see the sweat on their necks and their wild eyes. Eventually they tire of the game and turn off into the veld, farting and kicking up their heels in farewell.

How big he'd grown the day he went down to the kitchen again, his voice deep now, his heart unsettled, searching for his friends. But the women stopped braiding each others' hair, fell silent and covered themselves; him seeing it and knowing there'd be no more chasing him round the stove. He turned to the ayah now old and blind in her corner, standing before her long before she spoke. You don't know who you are, she said, and it makes the girls uneasy. It's time for the real work now, it's time for you to find your way; when you have learned what there is to learn you can come back here but you have to leave us first. In the corner of his eye the kitchen curtain moved and he followed it, turning, up the steps into inwardness, like a house where the shutters are closed at dusk and not opened again in the morning.

It was in that time of darkness he was told of his marriage. How the night tightened round him then, the ceremony trumpeted with dancing and parades, with soldiers elders relatives priests, and his father watching him for signs of happiness but there were none. The eyes of his tiny bride sweeping the ground as the conches blew, her tiny shoulders garlanded, his tunic layered in petals and him resigning to a life without surprise. Yasodarah – it was not her fault. He remembered the soft skin of their coupling, the chestnut eyes, the loquat nipples, and how she'd turned her face to the wall to escape his mute despair. How she'd danced to soften his loneliness then, bathed in rosemary, waited in her chamber for him to go to her again. But he never did and now it was her turn to sit in the kitchen with the ayahs and listen to their stories. How she'd found him in the colonnade and told him of the child inside her, defeated by his lack of joy. Now he heard again the weeping from her room, the otherworldly cries of birth from which he fled under the almonds and when the messengers came with the happy news they stammered at his silence and left him there in the blackness which the wild rejoicing could not reach, nor the wordless pleas of his wife and son in their empty bed. How she'd reached for him. How he'd looked away.

And there it was, the second woman to turn from him, one in death one in disappointment – and he knew he should have kneeled at her feet but couldn't. And now the sorrow rose to choke him, his swollen eyes staring at him from the mirrored puddles as his past peeled off whether he liked it or didn't, whether he was ready or wasn't, his lives hunting him down in the shadow of the ditch and it wasn't his life any more, it was the life of everything that had ever lived and everything that had ever died or that wanted to and couldn't.

So Siddhatta abandoned the house for the stables where his wild friend Channa worked and slept. And there the young men groomed the horses in their stalls, side by side in the uncomplicated heat and hay, brushing out the terrors of the night. Channa chattering like a mongoose about a life beyond the gate, about the games and fights and dancing there, the drunken singing, the willing girls; Siddhatta entranced and frightened. And when the house was closed that night they led the horse with sacking around his hooves past the guard asleep with wine or dreams. They mounted then with Channa holding on behind and clattered up the road at a gallop, whooping to get their spirits high, shouting into the wind, in among the houses, in among the mothers who smiled and shook their heads. But when Channa leapt to chase a squealing girl he left Siddhatta panicked in the saddle, sliding out of shape between the shacks. From every side came sickness, scorn and death, swollen bellies, empty cradles, shouts, blows, breaking pots and the rich young man on the handsome horse completely utterly lost. Siddhatta turned his head then and looked into the night and he knew he had seen what he could not forget, that now he knew nothing at all, and the expensive bridle with its pretty bells only made everything worse. A cry from the shadows shattered him into myriad pieces and the stallion found its own way home that night with him a disassembled man in the saddle still, the little bells still ringing.

All these memories swept through him now in the mud and slush – the young man in the fine house who fell into loneliness, the bleeding of the world held in his skin like a thorn. How no-one could reach him there, not the acrobats, jugglers, clowns, the magicians or physicians, not the anxious whispering aunts or his father's face bent over him, how he lay back on the flowered pillows looking at nothing for there was nothing to be seen.

But the kind and lively Channa was not done. He came to Siddhatta's sickbed then and clapped his hands. He dressed him and took him by the hand to the great pomegranate, where they climbed to the top to look out over the wall at the roofs and fields, into the yards where the children played and cats slept. And then the world breathed out and stopped. For beneath the young men swaying in the tree like falcons, a sage came stepping down the path, silent through the grass, with peace rising from his arms like lavender; one who didn't look away, one who touched the old man's face, the child's hair, who took the food in his begging bowl and walked back out of sight into the grove from where he'd come and now Siddhatta felt a joy coursing through his veins out into the vast blue sky. And he floated in the branches there with a lightness in his heart that he understood no more than the wind in his face. Ah my friend, he said.

Now nothing was in its place. At every step the pain and disappointment, at every step the hermit's radiance. Siddhatta knew what he had to do and he knew in a shaft of blackness he could not. But Yasodarah saw. And she stood before him with the child in her arm, lifting her hand to the side of his face. You'll never rest until you've found it, she told him, but you cannot do it here; go now and when you are ready we will come to you. He stepped back to refuse a love too great for him but the baby reached up and pulled his nose. He woke up and they wept.

He remembered now the night he left the house, walking over the drunken women to the nursery where he pulled back the curtain on those tiny dreams, on the little sleeping breath so slight he feared the boy was dead but he wasn't. How the sannyasin's face, his ayah's words and Yasodarah's gift rose and fell with the little blanket and he dropped the cloth and turned – the little boy's mother behind the screen, her hands across her mouth in case she cried out.

Now he was Gotama the yogi, who'd given a life away to find one. But he was a seeker whose penance burned with desperation, who drifted in trances with a restless mind, who fasted hungry, who bowed to teachers but found out nothing for himself. The new life never came. He had reached the end. Now, at last, there was nowhere left for him to go.

PART III
TEN THOUSAND MILES OF CLEAR BLUE SKY

The Great Way is vast – what's the rush?

– ADAPTED FROM THE *BOOK OF SERENITY*, CASE 28

I slow down into Fauresmith, past the rows of identical township houses, past the bottle store and the shop selling bread, firewood and fishing tackle. Fishing tackle? Fauresmith is a small Karoo town far from water, with a railway line down the street. The train doesn't run any more but I remember seeing it about twenty years ago.

I was organising a community rights meeting in the local hotel and had to use a back room because the participants were black – now the hotel is owned by a black businesswoman who allows whites in with a smile, as long as they drink her brandy. During the discussions there was a rumbling in the room as if something large was about to rise up from the floor. 'Oh it's just the train,' they said. But to me trains are elemental ancestral beings so I adjourned the meeting and stood in the street to watch the huge elegant creature come slowly toward me, transfixed by the sheer massiveness of its presence, by the rumbling engine, by the hot breath on my cheek as it passed, its weight shuddering the ground under my shoes. It must be like this to swim with a whale, I thought. When the meeting resumed, our concerns about life didn't feel quite as pressing as before, so we quickly sorted out what was important and went home.

However much accused persons swagger during a murder trial, when the moment comes to pronounce the sentence of death, everything changes. All at once they are vulnerable and human; now I am the last friend they have, the one who speaks for them, the one who brings them cokes and cigarettes. Of course the debate about the death penalty will continue forever. But no argument can take away the impossibility of reacting sensibly when the judge says to the person sitting beside me, 'You will be taken from here to a place of safety where you will be hanged by the neck until you are dead. And may God have mercy on you.'

One young man I defended came from outside Fauresmith; he was convicted of killing his uncle and sentenced to death. He wrote me a letter from death row where condemned prisoners were given a free rail ticket for a family member to visit them. He just wanted his mother to see him before he died. I went to his mother and she told me she would dance on her son's grave. In the end I told the young man that I was unable to find his mother but I was sure that, if she knew where he was, she would spare no effort to go to him. He was one of the last people to be hanged before the death penalty was abolished in South Africa. He, too, died utterly alone.

These things cut too deep for the partial world of opinion and judgement. In our hearts we can only stay open to the helpless unknowability of what this life truly is. However reprehensible the actions of persons sentenced to death, whatever arguments we support about judicial punishment, there is one thing I know in every pore of my being; that nobody is beyond the reach of love. Must I say it softer? Nobody...

As I drive past the old church out of town, I see an astonishing scene in my rear view mirror. Two women are fighting in the street. Their shirts are off and a crowd stands round them. One of the women rips her opponent's bra with a knife and she is executing a victory dance. A tall figure steps forward in an old-fashioned pill-box hat, the person with the knife runs away and the crowd vanishes. Two women stand in the road with their arms around each other – one elegant and upright; the other defeated, drunk and topless, holding in her body all the agony of the world.

Beyond the heartbreak
Open hills

The Fauresmith street fight has unnerved me and I am reminding myself to breathe slowly. Should I turn around to help? But I don't. A fierce debate about right and wrong unsettles me and I know I have lost the moment. So I turn right towards Philippolis, off the tar road with its railway track and potholes, onto the dirt. The dust rises in my rear view mirror like a tail, then settles again slowly.

Meditation teachers often use an analogy of mud settling to the bottom of a pond to illustrate the mind slowly clearing in meditation. But Zen Master Dae Gak likes to talk of dust settling on the gravel road after a car has gone past. I can understand that now.

Godwin liked to call himself a third class meditator. Croft tells me this came from a day when Godwin was travelling first class in a train in Sri Lanka and he missed his station so he had to get off at the next town and go back. But this time he was in third class. He was standing in the carriage complaining to himself when he realised he was the only person there who was unhappy and that he was unhappy because he was still travelling first class in his mind. That was when he decided to accept being third class and he had no more suffering. The people in the carriage around him were enjoying the noisy chaos of their lives and it made him laugh. Meditation is the same, Godwin said, don't expect things to be perfect and enjoy going third class.

The Jeep rattles over the corrugations onto a ribbon of clay. I ride quietly, soothed by the smoothness, by the gentle corn colour of the road, by its tinges of pink and purple. On every side the veld reaches to the sky and there are no buildings to break the horizon. After a week of legal disputes, I am quite alone again and the relief lifts my spirits. I hum a tune whose words I have long forgotten. Colourful Nguni cattle lie around a windmill near the road and watch me pass, chewing solemnly.

The third jewel in the Buddhist tradition is Sangha. Sangha means community. In the early days of the Buddhist order, it referred to the monks who walked with the Buddha from place to place, sleeping in groves outside the villages. Later, in a scandalous move, nuns were included. When Buddhism ripened into what is now called The Mahayana (the Great Way), lay people were added to the Sangha. Zen is part of the Mahayana, which emphasizes the ultimate emptiness or unknowability of everything, the interdependence of everything, and the practice of compassion towards everything. Finally, in the age of ecological awareness, we see that the Sangha includes the entire natural world – every tree, cloud, bird and beast of the field. And every tear that is shed.

Sangha can be the sense of mutual support among people who meditate together. It can be old school friends who meet to remember their innocence. It can be the itinerant shearers at the farm who pray each morning before work, or grandmothers in townships who gather little children in their shacks to feed them. It can be a family drawn together by a common history that goes beyond liking each other. It can be the difficult people in our life who challenge and test us till we want to strangle them. Maybe strangling someone is Sangha; maybe dying hand-in-hand in a locked garage is sangha. A sangha of two. Or it can be any one of us driving on a gravel road through an amphitheatre of far blue hills. Whatever form it takes, Sangha is the sense that we are all of us bound to each other in ways too intricate and infinite to understand and that we share this universe with each other.

I recently saw a documentary on Desmond Tutu as a young priest, in the days when black people were being removed from their homes in what the officials called 'white areas'. When he greeted a woman outside her tent in a forlorn resettlement camp in the Transkei, he met her with unreserved respect. When he spoke to the policeman who put her there, he met that person, too, with unreserved respect. This genuine respect freed the Reverend Tutu to debate, to disagree, to weep and to laugh. It is the fruit of a great and disciplined selflessness. We see it and we instinctively know it to be beautiful. Sangha.

Zen Master Dae Gak's young daughter spent a few days at the winter retreat. On the way to lunch he came up behind her and snatched her fluffy leopard-print hat off her head. Then she took his beanie and pulled it over her ears. She punched him on the arm. He bumped her with his shoulder. They put their arms around each other and walked off down the path.

The Jeep is happy now. It has the whole road to itself and I drive right down the middle. On each side there is a corridor of grass between the road and the fence which the wandering cart people used to call Die Langplaas – the long farm. Only a decade ago there were cart families living here at the roadside in shacks of tin and sack, the adults sitting on upturned paint tins among thin dogs while young boys herded the donkeys along the grass. In appearance they often had strong Bushman features – nut-butter skin, creased faces and high cheekbones. The farmers had a love-hate relationship with these wanderers, using them for hard manual work and blaming them for anything that went missing. But the carts have gone now. Die Langplaas is empty. The families have moved to squatter camps outside the towns where they swell the ranks of the unemployed and sell their donkeys for brandy. On Christmas day Margie and I still go out to the encampments with pots of meat but often there is a desperate fight over the gifts and we come home without speaking.

I turn on the radio to catch the news. There is nothing that interests me; more point-scoring by politicians, more chaos in international markets, more opinions on fracking in the Karoo. Fracking – the mining of shale for gas – is a big topic around here because the Karoo is a sensitive ecosystem with limited water. On the one hand, the debate is about money, energy and politics; on the other, it is about a place that evokes a mythic tenderness in the national psyche. The argument is fierce. I can't find my way through the myriad contentions and my wife is doing her best to educate me. In the meantime I will stay open to the true nature of this delicate landscape, I will drive through it as if I am driving through my own heart, I will remind myself that everything on this earth is transient, and I will drink in this beloved moment like a long draught of clear Karoo water.

After the news, my ears are caught by a melodious voice as a young presenter begins her afternoon talk show. She talks as if she is singing. Today's interview is with a man from the community of Orania which lies near here, over the hills to my right. Orania is the home of white Afrikaners who want to keep their traditional way of life intact in the new South Africa. It is a small town with its own currency, prim and litterless in the desert under the statue of a giant koeksuster. Of course the very existence of the place and all its stands for is a subject of more strong views, as the callers on the radio soon show her. I have some experience of Orania myself from my human rights days when I used to pick up white labourers hiking outside the town and take them to Hopetown to buy brandy; I liked the way they moaned about the arrogant white bosses and their refusal to pay proper wages or allow a bottle store on the premises. So I was interested to see if people's views had changed. They hadn't.

Everyone who phones in derides the people of Orania for their backwardness, for their stubbornness and for trying to keep apartheid alive under the guise of culture and tradition. The presenter listens without interruption, then asks naively, 'And where are you phoning from? Is it beautiful where you live? Are the streets lined with trees there?' The man from Orania does his best but it is clear nobody wants to listen to him. The young presenter offers no judgement, only an open ear. Gradually the callers are softened by her sympathy and something different emerges. A white woman wants the recipe for vetkoek. A Zulu man thanks the Orania spokesman for the respect he shows to callers of all races. By now I am so moved that I want to phone in myself. There is no cellphone reception here so I can't but, as I drive through the vast openness, it is like listening to birds singing in the branches.

Driving on gravel means driving attentively and I slow down to a
more leisurely speed. The road flows through the veld. It feels like
the face of an old friend, rough and full of character. Sometimes,
when the clay surface is smooth as silk, a hum begins to rise from the
undercarriage. It is faint and gentle, hardly there at all really, more
a presence than a sound. There is nothing that can be added to such
a moment to complete it, nor can it be held or owned. For at that
moment the earth, the wheels, the Jeep, the blue sky and myself are –
quite simply – in tune.

Dirt road
Clear mind

The Orania interview has finished now and the young presenter is tackling another fractious question; begging. In a country with so many poor people, it is a subject close to everyone's heart. Some callers are angry at being confronted with poverty at every traffic light and parking lot. Others offer impersonal solutions like soup kitchens and food vouchers. Then the presenter leans in to confide in us, floating her honesty like a balloon; 'You know, sometimes I want to blame poor people for being poor. But when someone comes up to me looking so desperate, I only see the pain and humiliation in his eyes and then I forget all the things I thought I should do.' That is it. Connection. At the level of judgement and opinion there is conflict at every corner. At the level of true connection it is quite simple. Young black men at the traffic lights sell hangers that nobody wants, white women in floppy hats stand doggedly in the sun guiding cars out of a parking lot. So we buy hangers we don't need, we tip car guards for a service we didn't want. Or we don't. To the anxious mind the way is impossible. To the open mind there is space and possibility.

My own experience of this comes from the ritualised begging practice in the monastery, though it had none of the despair that belongs to the truly poor. When I was a monk at Mt Baldy in California we were sent in pairs to the Los Angeles Fruit and Veg market to beg for food. By 3am we were in the monastery truck feeling our way down the switchback to the world below, past the corner where Shitty the Sewerage Man went over the edge and killed himself. By sunrise the market was already a vibrant place, awake while the world slept, pulsating with a loud uncomplicated energy that made me homesick for Africa. Young boys pushing barrows laden with yellow fruits, adults at the stalls teasing each other and shouting at the young ones to pack the oranges here and the bananas there. It was another world, a world of little English, a mix of races and faces, colours and fragrances.

This was the monks' begging ritual: we would stand in silence near the entrance of a stall in our robes, eyes on the ground, hands clasped over our stomachs with an empty sack over our arms. Sometimes the stall holders would nod at us, sometimes the boys would insult us affectionately – hey baldy mind your toes – but mostly we were ignored. It was difficult. And Sasaki Roshi insisted that we were not true monks if we did not taste the humiliation of waiting on the generosity of others. In Los Angeles there was none of the respect there is in a traditionally Buddhist country, where it is an honour to give to monks. So we stood and we waited, watching everything under our lowered eyes – the athletic steps of the barrow boys, the shuffle of agents, sometimes the cheeky clip of high heels followed by whistles of delight. Then someone would come to our elbow and whisper that they had a bag of old tomatoes that got spoiled or avocadoes too bruised to sell. And so we would slowly work our way into the stalls, coming out with fragrant dripping boxes which we stacked at a corner until there were enough to carry off to the truck. Of course we seldom got any good stuff, though there was a Korean man who would bow to us and offer a pallet of strawberries from his top shelf, 'Best for Buddha,' he said and we would bow to him in return. So that is what Roshi means, I realised one day – deserving nothing, I thank you from the bottom of my heart.

Then we would drive back through the city, stopping for donuts and coffee that made us so excited we jabbered like schoolboys all the way back to Mt Baldy. There the boxes were unpacked, the rotten pieces were cut out and the peels were put in the pot for the day's soup.

The Bushmen ancestry of the people around here looks out from every face. My friend Cait – who died too young – took up the Bushmen cause long before it became fashionable. She wanted a lawyer to find land where the Bushmen could live in their traditional way so she called me to a meeting on a desolate mountain transit camp. There I listened to animated men who made a wonderful story out of everything; they didn't ask for land, they just told me how there were no doves in the hills to which they'd been moved. I remember waking that night to the infinitely faint sound of a bow struck by a stick, a sound that seemed to come from the very stars themselves. I then asked my friend Roger Chennels to help with the project – the man who so endeared himself to Margie when he described *Stoep Zen* as a love story – and Roger went to meet his clients on the same mountain. Roger is a committed human rights lawyer. He is also a sceptic. When he was asked if he could help, he was not sure. Then one of the community leaders, a man with the name of Regopstaan – Stand-Up-Straight – took one of Roger's expensive city shoes and placed it on a rock. He told Roger that, if he hit the shoe with his arrow, Roger would be able to help them. Regopstaan walked off with his bow in his hands, turned and shot the tiny arrow straight into the shoe. At which the sceptical Mr Chennels resigned himself to his fate and became the Bushman advocate for many years. On a wall in his house there still hangs a shoe with an arrow wedged between the sole and the expensive leather upper.

I can feel my eyes becoming heavy so I pull over to the side of the road and lie back in my seat. I sleep instantly and wake ten minutes later, completely refreshed. The sky is still blue and I drive on.

Everywhere I turn
Ten thousand miles of clear blue sky

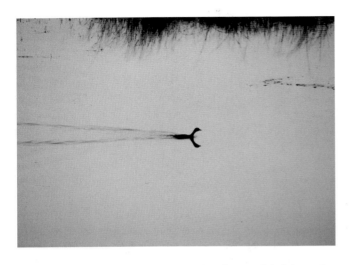

Little Freddie is one of the boys that come to the children's weekends at the farm. He tells Margie that the grown-ups in his house hit him when they are drunk and they are drunk every day, so he sleeps in the hen hut with his friends, the chickens. And he shakes. He shakes so much he can't hold a pencil. Because he can't write, he fails every year at school. A friend of ours donated drums for the children and Margie gave Freddie a drum to beat. Beating a drum is a bit like shaking and Freddie has found one thing he can do.

When Freddie came to the farm he sat in a circle with the others and hit his drum. During the breaks he ran in circles on the grass because he was so happy. On the last afternoon everyone got down on the floor of the zendo for a guided relaxation. Freddie and Margie lay next to each other. They all breathed slowly in and slowly out. In and out. Full and empty. Margie felt Freddie reach out and put his little hand in hers. And then he fell asleep.

They are playing music on the radio now and my presenter is probably having a cup of tea. I switch off. There's a horse cart ahead of me so I slow down and give it a wide berth. As I pass, I realise there is no driver – the horse is taking the cart home with nobody in it. I drive on past big-horned cattle at a dam and stop to tell two people sitting under a tamarisk tree that a free taxi is on its way to fetch them.

I loved it when people wrote to me about *Stoep Zen*. It made me happy. It still does.

Shortly after the book was published I was conducting arbitrations in Virginia, a gold mining town south of Johannesburg. One of the men I worked with was an Afrikaner from the mines, a former welder and an unapologetic racist. His name was Karel and he told everyone daily that the new South Africa was the end of him.

One day Karel called me to his office and waved the book in my face. 'And this?' he demanded, stabbing the cover with his finger. 'Stoep? Zen?' I laughed and owned up to writing it but didn't think it was quite his kind of reading. 'Oh no, my friend,' he said, leaning towards me, 'This book was written for me. Only for me, you hear? The bloody farmer who put his gun to the black's head – that's me. The policeman who kicked the black in the stomach – that's me. Ag no man. It's like looking into a bloody mirror – my friend, you've just buggered my life.' He looked at me. Under the belligerent affection something delicate rose up between us, something too delicate to be called by it's true name. So we put the book aside and talked about rugby instead.

When I turn the radio back on again, my friend is back. She is talking about Archbishop Tutu and his 80th birthday. She tells us about the archbishop's mother, who always took the side of the loser in an argument. I sit in my seat and smile with happiness at such fearless non-attachment. A group of springbok bounce away from the road, their white tails up, their feet pointing down like ballerinas. The presenter remembers how Tutu's secretary once asked him what it was like to do his annual meditation retreat; 'Oh,' said Tutu, 'It is like sitting in front of a warm fire on a cold winter's evening.'

One day we too will lie
Like leaves
At the bottom of the stream

Shunryu Suzuki Roshi famously said, 'In the beginner's mind there are many possibilities; in the expert's mind there are few.' When we make judgements, we close doors. We hold to our conclusions and shut down the vitality of the world. We create a world of boxes where everyone is frozen into the shape of their mistakes or into the shape of their successes. But if we can stay open then we grant others the space to change and grow; and we grant ourselves the same. It is not difficult, we just have to let go. Empty road, boundless mind. The possibility of waking up is present in every moment – for everyone. A secretary bird sails overhead and lands, running, on the far side of the fence.

The afternoon talk show ends and a sports announcer moves in behind the microphone. He talks about a rugby test between England and South Africa last summer. I remember the game because I wrote a story about it and gave it to my friend Kobus, a former dominee from Bloemfontein. Here is the story, as best I can remember it.

At the farm, when the Saturday rest is over it's time for rugby. I head out in the baking heat to the workshop where I look for something to do, then I tip out the screws onto the workbench and arrange them in sizes.

I turn on the little radio from the Gas and Braai shop, hang it from a beam to catch reception on the Afrikaans station. It is the end of the boeremusiek programme and the mood is set for the test between South Africa and England at Twickenham – a clash still ringing with emotions from the war with the British a hundred years ago, even if the Afrikaner's team is now dotted with black names the commentator can't pronounce. The screws are in their bottles and the bottles are in their places on the shelf. The radio swings gently in the heat. The concertinas bring on a generous mood so I pull out an old piece of planked cedar to make a shelf for my wife's collection of plastic shampoo bottles.

Nkosi Sikelel' iAfrica comes over the loudspeaker, distorted and muddled, sounding like the moan of trains on a shunting line at the railway sheds. By the time I have clamped the cedar in the vice, the English are having their turn and they sing God Save the Queen with one voice; the commentator is stirred – he is also embarrassed and assures us that we can kick the ball better than we can sing. I take the sharpening stone and the oils and set to work on the blade of the hand plane, drawing circles on the stone until the bevel glints. The game is not going well and the commentator's voice has a resigned air; maybe he feels how hot it is in the oven of the workshop. The blade begins to float on the stone – that change from bluntness into a keen edge, as subtle and clear as the moment somebody dies. The blade makes a fine slice on my thumbnail and I fit the plane together.

Now the English crowd is singing wildly and the commentator resorts to stock phrases from the war to keep his mood up – never surrender, last stand, outnumbered but brave – from which I gather the South Africans are losing badly. I go outside to the windmill and dip my head under the water.

The plank is squared off and I start to round off the front edge; the plane begins to bite but the rhythm is still breathless. In the second half there is a moment where the South Africans get the ball and swing it from side to side, sweeping forward from the left and from the right, towards the English line. The voice from the radio rises in pitch. I listen with the back of my ears, the plane in my hands gliding over the wood, shavings at my feet. The rugby comes and goes, the wood comes and goes; they begin to melt into each other.

South Africa forces a penalty and draws clear. The commentator is inspired. Now the wood begins to shine like glass, my body and the plane move as one. The Springboks run the ball from their own line and pass it from hand to hand like magicians and they score in the corner of their opponents' line. The man on the radio is so emotional I can't hear what he is saying, his words a torrent of gratitude to the black winger who has made him choke with joy and before my eyes a cream-coloured cedar shaving curls up from the plane into a spiral of perfect beauty, up and up, round and round like the shell of a tiny transparent snail. I lift it and hold it up to the light, my heart beating with astonishment.

Behind me the radio is pouring tributes to the heroes in green. A polka begins to chug happily from the little loudspeaker while I take the shaving to the door of the shed and let it go. It rises on the air like a butterfly and then floats off into the veld and out of sight.

Dominee Snyman became a minister in the Dutch Reformed Church. When he realised how white his heart was, he applied for a calling in a segregated black congregation in KwaZulu-Natal, where he was accepted without hesitation. At his inauguration in the Zulu community of Ulundi the dominee's father stood up in front of the crowd and said, 'I am an Afrikaner and I am too old to change. So today I give you my son, for you to teach him how to live in the new South Africa.'

The kind of effort we make in meditation is a bit like remembering something we have forgotten. We don't know where we put our keys and it doesn't help trying to remember because the trying trips us up. We have to stop trying. We have to trust that the genuineness of our question will allow the memory to rise by itself from the place it is hiding. Then, just when we are looking the other way, we know. We pick up the keys, start the car and drive on. That is meditation; you can't pin it down but, if you loosen your grip, it will find you.

There is dust ahead. I slow down. As I come over the hill there are men on horseback shouting, sheep dogs racing from side to side, and between them a flock of merinos trot along the road, leaving a carpet of droppings on the hoof-marked surface. The horses drive a wedge up the middle of the sheep and allow me to pass, the herders with their arms above their heads in greeting. I wave back from my glass cubicle, then tell myself there's more to life than a clean shirt and roll down the window. I turn off the engine. Dust drifts. Horses stand. The sheep mill around us and the dogs lie with their tongues out, panting. The men and I discuss the weather and they point to the dam beside a windmill where they are taking the young ewes. Because my Xhosa is so limited, we point and gesture and repeat ourselves; it doesn't matter, we are just sharing this moment for the joy of it. I start the car and leave them behind. We all wave for the last time. In my rear view mirror the sea of wool closes again behind me and I drive on. One life.

Here is another piece of doggerel written for Margie on her birthday.

From foreign lands they brought with them
Their holy bibles and their zen
Telling us to meet our maker
Cross our legs to meditate and
Vote a little later.

Then came nineteen-ninety-four
When some got less and fewer more
Things are now a little wilder
Farm kids still can't go to school
Cause no-one paid the driver.

Far from the insanity
We toast you with a glass or three
Of Merlot in the steaming bath
Toes around each other's ears
Me on the plug at the end of the year
And quite insanely
Laugh.

A tortoise crosses the road. I brake but not so close as to make him stop walking and pull into his shell. The inside of the Jeep fills with a fine dust. The tortoise doesn't need me. He just keeps on going with his primitive eyes, putting one foot in front of the other until he disappears into the grass.

As I start again I am seized by an unexpected happiness. Softened by the angelic radio presenter and the fearless tortoise, I begin to sing out loud with Tannie Betsie's picnic basket on the seat behind me – not as beautifully as the young petrol attendant but undilutedly me, the only voice in the universe, wild, wobbly and abandoned, bellowing half-forgotten childhood songs under an empty sky. I hold the steering wheel with my knees and slap the roof out the open window. The Jeep rocks. When the singing fades, I am alone again with the comforting creak of wheels on the gravel. My heart is beating and, to my surprise, I taste the salt of tears in the corner of my mouth.

I am so thankful I can fly.

As a lawyer of sorts, fairness is my game. When I have to decide a dispute, I listen respectfully to both sides and then make the fairest decision that I can.

But I know there is ultimately little fairness in life. 'Why didn't I get the long legs, the kind parents, eyes that can see?' The only level at which there is true equality is the place beyond fairness and unfairness. Beyond measurement, comparison, expectation; beyond winner and loser, victim and oppressor. Beyond equality. That is the house of God, the Buddha land. Emptiness. When we stop looking for fairness then nothing is unfair. There is only the fence alongside me at the edge of the road.

These poems that I write you
Don't worry if you're baffled by the words
Scan them with your fingers
Gently
The way a doctor searches for the pulse
Pick up, perhaps, in signals of excitement
The very rhythm beating in your heart

Someone is walking down the road swinging her arms, a woman in a long grey skirt with nothing in her hands. I stop and open the door. She climbs in, we ride on. But when I ask where she is going so far from anywhere, she turns to me and smiles. She is going to her sister in Philippolis who has had a new baby. But that is far? Yes it is far and she turns again to the front. She is like my friend Chambers who lives in a small town notorious for its poor streets. One morning he opened the door for a friend and was greeted by a tirade about the terrible potholes and the stupid government. 'Yes the potholes are big,' said Chambers, 'Come inside.'

In the koan dialogues of the early Zen Masters in China, Master Chou was brilliant at doing the same thing. Whenever he was confronted with an opinion from the world of preferences or a question that smelled of Zen he simply responded with what was in front of him. One day he was sweeping the floor when a monk asked him, 'Great Master, you have such wisdom, so how can there be dust?' Chao Chou said, 'It blows in from outside.' Don't get caught in the opposites, our own or those of others. Keep it ordinary. Keep it concrete. Then you can follow the True Way down the dirt road from Fauresmith to Phillippolis.

I think of all the conflicts and intolerance around religion and they make me sad. I remember walking into the zendo one evening to find Margie busy with the little wooden Buddha figure on the altar that our friend Louis gave us from Indonesia. What are you doing? I ask. Rubbing his tummy she says. Very clear.

 Although we tell people we don't worship the Buddha, some people have a devotional quality in their heart that can't be kept down. Margie is one of them. Our house is littered with saints, Buddhas, bishops, ancestors, puppies, umbrellas, urns and godchildren. Margie happily makes sure they are comfortable, chatting away to them about her day. She doesn't see any contradiction in these ancestors from different traditions. At that level of selflessness, there isn't any.

133

In South Africa separation and mistrust eat into our bones. They have been built into our childhoods, passed down to us in countless gestures of fear and disrespect. Then came the dismantling of the Pretoria regime and the remarkable leadership of Mr Mandela. How we all hoped that our loneliness would die with apartheid. Instead, at the very moment when we thought a redeemed life was in our reach, new kinds of separation and suffering sprang up. At the level of public discourse, it is difficult not to be disconsolate. But, if we look beyond our anxiety, we can also see something else. On the streets, in the pubs, in the corridors of parliament and pews of churches, on athletics tracks and in rehearsal halls, people are building a new country far from the public gaze. Sometimes brilliantly, sometimes badly, but all part of this great process.

In our anxiety we are always asking ourselves how things are going here. But if we answer, 'well,' we have forgotten the tears; if we answer, 'badly,' we have lost the tune. The problem has a false bottom and we can't answer in terms of the question itself – we have to go beyond the duality of good and bad into something else. More like the way we look at a painting or listen to a piece of music. More like a Zen koan which calls us out of our partial life into something greater. Only then will the question cease to haunt us and we will be able to live here – or anywhere – with enthusiasm, wisdom and gratitude.

I wept and asked myself
What have I done with the garden entrusted to me?

I pull over to the side of the road and climb out, slowly stretching my body and breathing in the warm air. In the middle of the road I stand and pee, drawing a pattern in the dust. Beyond the fence an anthill has been hollowed out by an aardvark. A soft breeze touches the tops of the grass and a lark comes to sit on the sneezewood post. He tilts his head to one side as he watches me. I watch him back. In the vast silence there is only a dim ringing in my ears and then, far and faint, the bleating of a sheep. I lift my heart to the sky and my eyes to the hills. I turn in a slow circle, drinking in the peace on every side. There is nothing other than this.

The third Divine Abode is Sympathetic Joy. This is a generous, airy quality. Like all the abodes, it rises naturally out of a life where we are not separate. Our hearts are open, so when people are happy we are happy with them. When they succeed we celebrate with them. When good things happen we are pleased for them. Most of all, when someone is clear and free – even for a moment – we rejoice with them, for that is surely the greatest happiness.

The people sing and the state president dances. I hear a man whistling in the public toilet and hum his tune as I go out.

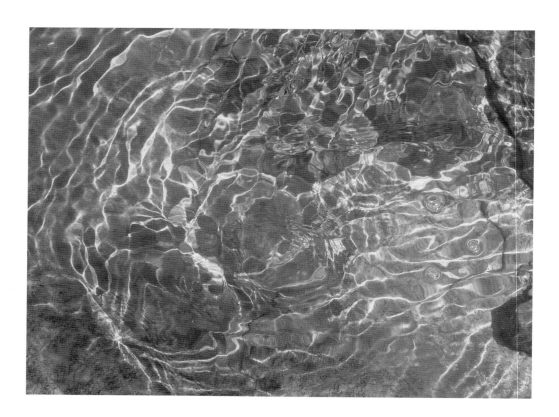

Philippolis lies near the Gariep river. Its back streets are lined with small Victorian homes that enchant the tourists and on the other side of the dry riverbed lies a desolate township. It is the birthplace of Laurens van der Post, the controversial writer and explorer who introduced the Bushmen to the western world – the man who was once chided for not being able to hear the singing of the stars. I met Sir Laurens once for tea on a mail boat between England and Cape Town. He was kind and formal, telling me that if he did not get back to the Karoo each year his soul became sick.

Philippolis was also once the home of the Griqua people. When they lost their lands, some stayed as labourers on white farms or as cart people on the back roads. The rest trekked east over the Drakensberg in search of a place they could call their own. Both stories ended sadly.

The error is profound
There's no place to look for it
Gods and humans together on dry land

The decisive moment for the Ch'an tradition in China was when the sixth patriarch, the illiterate southerner Hui Neng, won a poetry competition set by the fifth patriarch to determine his successor. The monks were asked to write a poem which would demonstrate their insight into Zen. The head monk and front runner Shen Hsiu wrote: 'The body is a Bodhi tree, the mind a mirror tall. Carefully we wipe them clean lest dust on them should fall.' Everyone looked at the verse, nodded at the great wisdom of it and returned to their meditations. Then the young kitchen boy Hui Neng asked someone to write on the wall his response to Shen Hsiu, which went: 'There's no such thing as a Bodhi tree or a mirror tall. Originally there's nothing so where can dust fall?' The fifth patriarch secretly recognised the wisdom of Hui Neng's poem and gave him the patriarchal robe and bowl in the middle of the night. But such were the politics of the day that he also advised Hui Neng to run for his life as the monastic powers would never agree to such a person as his successor. Hui Neng took the robe and bowl and ran.

I love the idea of choosing a leader by the poems he or she writes. As a conscientious Zen student, I dutifully tried the mirror-polishing kind of Zen and ended up with damaged knees. I tried the everything-is-empty kind of Zen and landed up borrowing cash and soap from friends. Now I just do my best with everything and try to keep my direction clear. Sometimes there is dust, sometimes not; sometimes there is clarity, sometimes not. So, in truth, I can only go back to what I know – that when I get home I will take a cloth and wipe the dashboard until it is clean again.

Vast Emptiness
Nothing Holy

Now the veld slopes down towards the Orange river. I laugh at the memory of a canoe trip down the river with my brother Maeder and some friends. The two of us were in one canoe, in the other was a psychiatrist who was a very public atheist and with him a dominee from town. Downstream from the dam wall Maeder and I pulled out at a heavy rapid but the others went straight into the boiling waters, exploding through the foam, shouting unheard above the roar. They made it through the rapid into the still pond on the other side and lifted their arms in triumph. But they hadn't seen the whirlpool. We held our breath as the back of the canoe disappeared under the water, as they climbed to the nose that was beginning to turn. The world was all silence. Then – we still don't know how – the two of them broke the spin and made it to the bank. There the dominee sank to his knees and thanked God for his deliverance, while the psychiatrist cursed the universe for throwing him into the jaws of death.

So who was right? Go beyond right and wrong then whirlpools will never defeat you. The believer and the atheist save each other on the nose of their tiny boat.

I look into your face
A gentle breeze blows across my cheek

The Jeep slows down on the bridge over the great river. Once again I stop. It is late afternoon and to my right the sun is lowering itself into the water, the willows on the bank motionless over the still surface. I walk to the side of the bridge and look down. The rocks are black and volcanic. On one of them a man is sitting with a fishing rod. The man, like the rock, is absolutely still. I pick up a stone and throw it into the water, wishing grace and blessings on all this beauty. The stone disappears. I am not far from home now.

Now he heard again his baby's cry in the long night, the tiny reaching arms he never filled. And he ached for all the trust undone, for the lonely, the sick, the forgotten and despised, for hearts broken by disappointment and longing, for stillborn calves and ducklings pecked to death and his heart swelled and burst and he vowed to attain enlightenment for the sake of  *all those in pain, not to waste another moment in putting right his wrongs, to return joy and peace to the world.*

The bikkhu opened his eye then and saw a beetle scrambling up the bank, he saw it fall on its back then turn and keep on coming, scuttling over his empty belly, his hollow ribs, across his empty chest along the skin of his outflung arm all the way to his wrist where it jumped off onto the path and disappeared. And if he'd a voice with which to cheer he'd have cheered for his tiny friend who kept on going but he couldn't. Instead, his heart opened as if the sun had come out between the trees and shone on him. It was then he knew he was not finished yet, that there was work to be done for the beetle and for him and for the love of it all he couldn't remember the difference between them apart from all those little legs. And in that knowing a small soft voice was calling that he almost heard and while the words eluded him there glowed inside him something new and bright.

That was when he heard – or maybe felt – feet threading towards him on the path and with them a sweet humming, bird-like in the air, a fragrance closing in on him and then it stopped, in the silence of which the thrushes rang their evening bells and a frog in the ditch called somewhere near his head. Eyes. Two almond eyes. A young face tilting to the side to see him better, to see that wreckage in the mud that was him. He thought how disreputable he must look and the thought made him smile though it hurt and she smiled back and they smiled at each other and she tried to pull him by the elbow but the skin came away in her short dark fingers and she stepped back in fright, him lying there bereft and above him a moth left the twisted mango branch and rose into the light and he with it.

That night it rained, rained in the dark. The drops fell gently through his bloodied lips, the wetness on his swollen tongue and Gotama gave himself to the infinite good fortune of his life as the water slid through the holes in his gums where the teeth should be, where it was cool beyond measure and he wondered if a man could be as happy as he, all the penance washed away in the kindness of that young face and in the rain that ran in sheets through his matted hair over his neck into his ears until the ditch began to fill around him, leaves and twigs to rise, he thinking mildly that he may drown there in that sweet torrentuous heaven and then the rain stopped and he lay there baptised and clean in the quiet.

She came again in the morning with her bowl of milk for the gods but you can have it she said because you've got eyes like a puppy. So she sat on the side of the ditch with her feet at his shoulder and slipped her hand under his head, lifted his awful face and between his lips she tipped the precious juice until the sweetness of it filled him and he let it slide down his stiffened throat and thanked her with his eyes and she wrinkled her tiny nose and put his head back in the mud and left him.

Then from the forgotten corners of his life there rose the memory of lying on a blanket under the wild apple, the maids running off to watch the ploughing and he in grateful solitude. The little boy straightened his back then, pulled his legs towards him, crossed them and drew into his belly the dappled air. As his breath came and went a peace fell upon him there beneath the leaves, the light whispering in his lap, and beyond that the crickets, birds and small far voices and there was nothing he did not feel as himself. Into this contentment ran a tiny mouse with panting sides and panicked eyes clean over the boy's folded legs and he cried out, 'Run run run I won't tell!' and how the little mouse had hurtled away to safety and him there smiling. Now, as he lay in his ditch remembering the boy under the tree, he knew the way was simpler than he'd ever dared believe, and more like kindness. So when the girl came to him again and lifted his head to feed him he gave himself up like a child, allowed her softness to cleanse him, and he with nothing to give her or teach her was born again in her gentle fingers and if he had tears to cry he would have cried there in her lap.

And so the world tumbled into clarity around him – him drowning in her hands as in his ditch, without name or rank, at one with every tender touch, with every heron, coot and ibis, robeless and holy in the fragrant mud with nothing left to seek and into the clearing came a pair of spotted deer to drink from the water in which he lay.

PART IV
HOME

'Alas, you've been travelling these roads too long.
It is all so clear but you still don't see it
so you get lost instead. Enough now!
Put your feet up beside the fire and rest.'

– ADAPTED FROM THE *BLUE CLIFF RECORD*, CASE 44

Soon he could lift his head to watch her skipping across the path, her skirts flying, mesmerised by the life in her, by the playfulness that no more saw itself than the squirrels in the branches. She lay on the fallen trunk squashing mangoes with her toes as he slept without dreams and when he woke she was gone. He lifted his eyes to the parrots and his heart to the sky in which they flew and knew that his new life was altogether different, different as light from dark though it came from the dark and she was there sometimes and gone sometimes and one morning she stood there above him her knees scratched from playing. Get up she told him, time to get up and he knew she'd not take no for an answer. Together they pulled and heaved, complaining protesting panicking groaning, scolding bossing giggling wheezing fussing, dragging him over the edge until the two of them lay helpless on the bank, bubbles of laughter lifting into the air – she the child she was, he the child he'd never been.

Day by day his strength grew under her soft butter and her gentle hands. When he tried to stand he fell and she laughed at him and he laughed at him and they never gave up until he was wobbling upright like a baby, his hands out in front of him in delight as he moved first one foot then the other, her clapping and whispering come to me come and him staggering into her small arms and her great heart. Each day he stood, each day he took more steps, until he could shuffle along the way beside the ditch where he had lain down to die. And she would look at him and throw her sticks into the air and catch them while he balanced himself in this great new wave of love and he wished his father could have been so happy. She listened to his story of Yasodarah's gift and laughed about the boy who'd pulled his nose; very soon, she said, they'll come to find you and he was grateful for the thought.

One day she told him about the great fig tree, the tree she loved more than anything, whose great wide branches she climbed, to whom she told her secrets, and he knew at once he would end his journey there. So he hardened the soles of his feet, walking up and down the path in the shade while she brought him food each morning like a mother would. Late on the day of the full moon she came from her home again to find Gotama washing in the ditch. She watched him take his robe and wrap it around his body, each careful movement ringed with peace. Then he knelt before her, holding her face between his hands. 'It's time,' she whispered. So he rose and she turned to stand beside him, slipping her fingers up into his. The two of them set out toward the setting sun, towards the tree; the thin man the tiny girl, side by side on bare feet, each step new and beautiful, their shadows tall behind them as they walked to a place that no-one had walked before.

South of the river the road is rougher. We are in a different province with a different department of roads. I steer from side to side, as I did at the start of the journey, but I'm more weary now and it is not as much fun. That's fine. Everything comes, everything goes. I pass the vet's rooms where dejected horses stand in the twilight. Someone has lit a fire outside for the evening that has not yet come; he stands before it very still, just watching.

Many years ago a family of cart people stayed at the farm to build a loading ramp. Barend Barends and his three sons Benjamin Barends, Benny Barends and Benji Barends lifted stones all day while their stick-like mother and her three daughters-in-law walked the veld for herbs. At the end of the week the ramp was done and the sons passed their wages on to their father; he gave them each a few coins for tobacco from the farm store. That night we were woken by the sound of drunken revelry at the cottage. Margie went down to see what was going on and I turned over back to sleep. When I next woke, the singing and shouting were still in full voice but Margie wasn't back so I pulled on a coat and shuffled down the path to the noise. This is what I saw: The three daughters-in-law are passed out in a heap around the fire. Barend Barends is on a chair playing a guitar with three strings while Benjamin, Benny and Benji sway in front of him, their arms around each other, singing too loud to hold the tune; every time their singing fades, Barend swears at them for being worse than jackal preying on his goodness and they revive. And there, two dark figures against the flames, Margie and old Mrs Barends dancing arm in arm to the three-string guitar.

When Godwin taught meditation, he would end the meditation period and allow time for questions. If someone asked him a question, he responded graciously and patiently. If nobody spoke, he stayed silent, with his arms folded across his chest and his eyes closed until it was time to leave. Then he would smile and say, 'Good discussion.'

One day, during Godwin's last visit to South Africa in 2000, I got a telephone call from Cape Town and heard his familiar soft voice. 'I just want to tell you I am not so well,' he said, 'So I thought I would like to speak to you and find out how your two small daughters are.' I knew Godwin suffered with his kidneys and I asked him if he thought his illness may be serious. 'Oh no,' he laughed, 'It's just living and dying.' That was the last time we spoke and within a month Godwin was dead. He was an extraordinary man and an extraordinary teacher, deeply beloved by all who were fortunate enough to meet him.

Blikkies is another throwaway child from the squatter camp. He doesn't know who is father is, his mother left for the city and never came back. He only goes to school when a neighbour takes pity on him and washes his clothes; when he gets there his eyes are too poor to read so he sits at the back of the classroom where the teacher won't notice him. Blikkies came to the farm for a children's weekend and Margie found that he could sing; he could sing in a voice so sweet and pure it made her cry – hymns and psalms that he heard in the church, tunes without words because the words were for the people inside. That night Margie asked him to show the others what he could do and Blikkies sang for them his wordless songs. His friends sat on their beds and listened to him and when he was finished they turned over and fell into their dreams. Margie went to say goodnight, she bent over Blikkies and kissed him on the forehead. She told him that any time he felt lonely he could remember the farm and how the children all listened to him. 'And aunty Margie,' he whispered, 'If I sing really good maybe my mama will hear me and come back home.'

I am driving in shadow now. It is the shadow of Colesberg mountain, Coleskop, that looms high above me in the west. The summit was used by English forces during the Anglo-Boer War to fire on the boers far below. I find myself wondering at the commitment of the English soldiers, hauling canon parts and iron balls to the top of the mountain with ropes and assembling them in the heat. How they must have cheered when the first shot went off! How far they were from home in their sunburned faces.

And far from home is where I found myself in the presence of my first Tibetan lama, Kalu Rinpoche, in Scotland so many years ago. The meeting went something like this. Interpreter: 'You have asked for an interview. Do you have any question for the Lama?' 'No.' 'Do you have anything you want to say to the Lama?' 'No.' Then a little conversation between the interpreter and the Lama. 'The Lama asks why you want to see him?' To my embarrassment I cannot find anything to say. I look into a face more full of wrinkles than a Bushman's. And it slowly unfolds into a smile, like one of those loose-skinned dogs getting up to stand. 'The Lama says you are far from home,' said the interpreter, 'He wants you to look after yourself and not worry so much. He says everything is always alright.'

In the Indian mythology of the time, the coming of a Buddha was a cosmic event because a Buddha – and there was more than one – is a being higher than the gods. So the Pali scriptures give a wonderful mythical account of all the trials levelled against Shayamuni by Mara the tempter as he took his seat under the Bodhi tree. This much we all already know from our own lives – that when we step into the field of selflessness, all the defences and strategies of the ego begin to arm themselves; for our small self, this is truly a matter of life and death and we underestimate its cunning at our peril. So Mara gathers his armies and attacks the Buddha-to-be with strength and guile, with flattery and aggression, with temptations of worldly power, celebrity and long-legged women. As the night deepens, Shakyamuni manages to shake free of them; the freedom that he has glimpsed is now more attractive than any of the temptations on offer.

Then comes Mara's last trick. But this is not another variation on the same theme; it is the temptation of self-doubt. 'Who do you think you are?' he demands to know. 'You want to be a Buddha? Bah! Just look at you, you spoiled rich boy – you disappointed your father, you walked out on your wife and your baby, you never held a job, you gave up on your gurus and now you think you deserve to be special?!' This was the final test – you are just not good enough.

Mara's question was Shakyamuni's koan. But it is a question each one of us has to confront every day. In answer, we want to avoid our faults and assert our goodness, we want to know we are okay; this is all part of the hook on which we dangle. In truth, the only way to resolve the dilemma is to go beyond being good enough or not good enough. So what does the Buddha do? He leans forward and touches the earth with his hand. He doesn't argue. He doesn't defend his worth. He just gathers his whole being into expressing what his life is at that very moment – Aah, the ground is soft and damp. How wonderful! The earth bears witness to his clarity.

It is at that moment, so the Pali scriptures tell us, that the trees in the forest drop their leaves at his feet, husbands and wives stop arguing and the moon smiles like a maiden filled with drink. Each of us, when we respond with our whole being, is worthy beyond measure. And it was only then that Mara fled, for there was nowhere left for him to stand.

The Zen version of the Buddha's awakening is different. And helpful in a different way. It was mentioned in *Stoep Zen* but it is worth repeating here. According to the Zen version of the story, Shakyamuni sat under the Bodhi tree in deep meditation, then he lifted his eyes and saw the evening star. That is it. Just that. As Zen Master Yunyan says, 'Just like this is It.' Just-like-this means everything appears to us moment by moment, as it is, in its 'suchness'. Each moment is complete. The star is just the star. The road ahead is just the road ahead. When we are awake enough not to add anything, then we know for ourselves how rich life is. And we can stop trying so hard to make something special out of it. Enough, as my mother used to say, is enough.

Through jewelled eyelashes
The evening star

It was not long after my meeting with Kalu Rinpoche, when I returned to the Easter school term at the cathedral, that I was at a service presided over by the Metropolitan Anthony of Sourozh, Archbishop of the Russian Orthodox Church in Exile in Great Britain and Ireland – surely one of the best titles in church history. Metropolitan Anthony is one of my great ancestors, the man who told a woman complaining that she couldn't pay attention during meditation that she should forget about meditation and take up knitting – and give every stitch to God. The archbishop gave a sermon in his rich bass voice, a sermon that filled me with a new and wordless understanding. Then, as he delivered his blessing in that vast old building, I completely disappeared, only to find myself back a lifetime or a few short moments later with his voice still ringing through the church.

The Lord bless you and keep you.
The Lord make his face to shine upon you and be gracious unto you.
The Lord lift his countenance upon you and give you peace.

Ouma Jas walked in the footsteps of her Lord. We all thought she may be a bit law-bound about it until we heard a story she never told her children. She used to visit the local old-age home as one of her Christian duties, always making time to speak to a terminally ill man known only as Mr Benjamin. Not only was it suspected that Mr Benjamin was secretly a Jew in a Methodist home but, when Ouma Jas leaned over his bed one afternoon to ask him if there was anything he would like, Mr Benjamin whispered that he would love a beer. As far as we know, Ouma Jas had never been inside a bottle store in her life except to haul some startled husband home to look after his children. But that same afternoon she returned to Mr Benjamin's bedside where she pulled out of her handbag a quart bottle of beer. 'Big handbag,' said Mr Benjamin.

At the side of the road a young man strides hatless. He moves freely, like a dancer, swinging his hips. I name him George Fox, for his beauty. George Fox was the founder of the Quaker tradition in seventeenth century England, the man who said that his life's work was to walk cheerfully over the earth, greeting that of God in everyone.

When the Buddha travelled from town to town, he usually lived in the groves on the outskirts. And he would be invited to dine with important persons in the town, eating at their homes with their families. It was part of the Buddha's begging practice so he ate what he was given – the Buddha was not a vegetarian, he was a monk.

The servants fluttered, father bathed
The plants were watered, the windows washed
Mother combed my hair.
Another guest from the jacaranda grove
Beyond the edge of town.

The little silver dinner bell called us to the table
To the low adult voices
The greetings
The blessings
Me and the pets invisible
Head down, ears up.
Then food came on trays with a sweep of skirts
The conversation fading away into
The scrape of spoons
small coughs
And outside two barbets in the mango tree.

His silence swelled into the room
More at home there than us.
It wasn't the patience or the care of his eating
That I saw there
It was just that nothing else existed
In the entire world –
Pushing the bones to the side of his plate
Cutting the butternut down the middle
Hands delicate as pearls.

It was then that I lifted my face
To be caught in two dark eyes of infinite ease
As
In a single stroke
He swept the chop
Under the table for the dog
And winked.

I reach the outskirts of Colesberg, the little town so delicately hidden in the koppies. I pass the house of Ouma Jas. I pass the bottle store that was once the law clinic. I pass the museum. At this late hour there are still cars and trucks on the street – it must be the end of the month when pensioners and farm workers come to buy rations and a lottery ticket.

I drive up Church Street amid a lively and chaotic congregation of hawkers, cellphone vendors and preachers. I can hardly see through my windscreen, it is so covered with dirt stuck to the entrails of insects. Sweetfields funeral parlour is advertising a special this week: You pay one, We bury two. Colesberg was once the northernmost point of the Cape colony. People and wagons passed through here on their way north, to the diamond mines and the gold mines and beyond them to the African interior; now the holiday classes from Johannesburg are coming down through the town to the sea. In the nineteenth century the racial planning of apartheid was not yet in place and the town had a famous black mayor in the imperialist David Arnot – the man who fired the pistol to start the weekly horse race and who sent meticulously labelled crates of succulents to Kew gardens outside London. Then, as in every little town in South Africa in the 1960s, the black and coloured residents were moved out of the town centre into the surrounding hills, from where they are now taking back the place, beginning with the pavements. And, once again, we have a black mayor. The history of the country is in its street, its koppie, its cemetery and its blue sky.

On a roadside barrow
Yellow oranges

Outside the Colesberg railway station there is an old church with tin walls and a tin roof. It is the local pigeon clubhouse. At a time of strict segregation of social activities, pigeon racing was the only multi-racial sport in the district, run by people who didn't have a politically correct bone in their body; men and women who argued over breeding and pedigree and willingly lost money every week on the birds. At club meetings the members still sit in the wooden pews under framed photographs of famous pigeons with puffed-out chests, bird ancestors with names like Freddy van Zyl the Fourth, Mrs Roux's Lost Husband and Miss Pamela Anderson.

I get a few supplies from the Railway Café on the corner where a mother and daughter in curlers are standing at the bread rack, already in their gowns and slippers. They are laughing at some private joke and everyone around them is watching, wondering what is so funny. But the humour is infectious and everyone walks out smiling.

Shadows on the track
Words in the heart
Neither leaving the slightest trace

Colesberg loves festivals. This year they held a catapult festival, where the local scrap metal dealer Piet Yster made a three-storey high metal catapult that never worked. There used to be a Harley Davidson bike rally each winter where the bikers would drink the town dry, where Fanie Foss the traffic cop would close off the main street with barricades so that the bikes could ride up and down in front of the Central Hotel. After a woman on the back of a motorbike took her top off during a 180 degree wheelspin outside the church, the organising committee decided to have a bicycle race instead.

Then there was the annual sheep festival that ran for a number of years and was widely thought to be a success. The street was filled with visitors and sheep droppings, there were sheep-shearing and sheep-counting competitions and under the trees were church stalls with boiled brains and roasted eyeballs. Each year there was some kind of musical entertainment in the evenings – local Afrikaans gospel singers, church choirs (they weren't a great hit), and once, rather desperately, when Max the Magnificent had to cancel his magic show, a dancer with the name of Cutiepie. Some of the committee members had their doubts about the picture in the newspaper but they were reassured on the telephone by Miss Cutiepie's mother who sounded a good woman. So Miss Cutiepie was flown down from Johannesburg in a private plane by Knyp Schutte in a journey that, everyone agreed, took far longer than they expected. The reception committee stood in the veld as the plane circled the Colesberg airfield and out stepped a young girl with peroxide hair and a ring in her belly button. By now doubt was surfacing again but it was too late.

That night in the town hall, after an opening prayer from the minister, the audience heard the opening bars of The Pink Panther theme tune and the girl from the aeroplane slipped her gartered leg through the gap in the curtains. The young farmers clapped and spilled their drinks. Encouraged by the enthusiastic reception, Miss Cutiepie stepped down into the hall in a belly dancing outfit and got Mr Erasmus the prison gardener to squirt shaving cream on her chest. The men went wild and Mr Erasmus bowed. In all the excitement Cutiepie's top came off and was thrown around the room. It was at this point that the treasurer of the organising committee phoned the police station but got no reply. She raced to the station in her 1400 Datsun but the only person on duty was the cleaner who told her that all the policemen were at the concert in the town hall.

I pull into the petrol station to fill up for the last stretch home and to clean my windscreen. The young man who comes to the car is the son of an old friend; at the law clinic I once kept his father out of jail and he has never forgotten. 'Welcome back uncle,' he says and inspects me closely. My face, like the windscreen, has a layer of fine sand from driving with the window down and he clicks his tongue at my neglect. He squirts soap over the window. He rubs at the greasy spots. As he pulls the rubber of the windscreen cleaner over the soapy glass his face appears before me, clear and radiant.

Then the young attendant opens the door and takes my hand. 'I want you to meet my friend,' he says and he walks me over to the Rastafarian man in dark glasses who sells wire windmills at the garage entrance. We all shake hands. The little windmills tinkle in the breeze. Then we talk about Bob Marley, which is about as much as I know of his tradition. 'You are a wayfarer,' says the Rastafarian solemnly, 'A pilgrim on the great way home.' I ask him if he makes windmills for Lord Jah. 'No,' he says. 'Every windmill is made just for you.' Victoriously, he grins. There is not a tooth in his mouth. I buy a windmill for my wife, we shake hands once more and I go back to my car.

We move through this life by means of our normal, conventional, common-sense self. But when we hold too tightly to who we think we are, when too much revolves around protecting and enhancing this self, we create great stickiness. We get stuck everywhere – in materialism or ascetism, security or insecurity, oppression or victimhood; and they all lead to suffering because they are all rooted in attachment to self. We have to go beyond these dualities into something else entirely. Something with no edges. Something far more risky. More selfless. More open.

What this something else is cannot be neatly defined; in fact, the very search for a definition is also part of our insecure self's futile attempt to render this world safe and comfortable. We know selflessness because we instinctively recognise it in ourselves as well as in others. We recognise it in inspiring public figures – in people like Mahatma Ghandi, Nelson Mandela, Martin Luther King Jr, Desmond Tutu, Jonathan Jansen. And the Dalai Lama of Tibet, Thich Nhat Hanh of Vietnam and the late Mahaghosananda of Cambodia. We see it in the private lives of women who look after orphans in the townships, of men who rise in the middle of the night to go to work for their family, of a friend with cerebral palsy who spends the whole morning trying to pull on his shoes. And we know it from moments in our own lives – in our sitting up all night with a sick child, in forgiving someone who has hurt us, in listening to a voice so beautiful it makes the night shine.

All these things are – as the late Shunryu Suzuki Roshi said – letters from the world of enlightenment. We can't define that world but we can smell it. We can't say what moves us but we are moved. Right there is the wellspring of genuine freedom, of true compassion, love and fearlessness. Right there is the taste of our true home.

I head out of town toward the Oorlogspoort turn-off. It has been raining and the potholes are puddles. Mud-spattered tipper trucks stand in a row at the road works. The construction workers have gone home but hikers stand along the road carrying cardboard signs to show where they are going – Port Elizabeth, Steytlerville, Mossel Bay. One woman's sign reads 'Moscow' and I am tempted to give her a lift as a reward for her sense of humour. But I don't. Instead, I hurry past, showing with my hands that I am about to turn off. I go left onto the gravel and over the railway line where I used to stand with the girls and wave at the train drivers. There is a song on the radio that I can't quite hear because I'm going out of range now, the scent of home in my nostrils. I say goodbye to the lady on the radio. And I remember that train drivers always wave back.

The fourth Divine Abode is Equanimity. In a sense, equanimity holds within it the other qualities of generosity, compassion, and sympathetic joy. It is the kind of even-mindedness that comes from being at home with all of life – with its difficulties, terrors and disappointments, with its ease and its contentment. At home with our flaws as well as our strengths. Not asking others to make us happy. Equanimity does not depend on going to church or joining a Zen group, on holding any particular belief or wearing robes. It does not depend on anything. Equanimity is what is left when you drop everything. Once everything has been put down, it can all be picked up again, freely and fearlessly swung over our shoulders. Then we can walk with it – light, balanced, contained. We can meet each person with respect, whoever they may be. As dignified as the woman walking on the side of the road with a suitcase on her head.

Around the bend near Klapfontein I pass a group of young farm boys and girls. I stop. The children pile into the back seat, giggling and pushing. They put Tannie Betsie's picnic basket carefully into the boot. I tell them the Jeep won't go unless they sing me a song. They giggle. We sit. Then a young girl begins to hum a hymn from the morning assembly, the others join in and soon the car fills with voices. The Jeep starts. I drive on with my heart overflowing.

As the sun sinks I remember something that happened when I was the monk in charge of the kitchen at Mt Baldy. I was up in the middle of the night kneading bread when I felt a sharp pain in my abdomen. It got so bad that I fell to the floor, leaving the dough on the counter. The kitchen at the monastery is far from the other buildings so I couldn't get up to ask anyone for help – and, of course, there were no cellphones in those days. Eventually I crawled on my hands and knees to the office where there was a telephone and woke up a friend to come and fetch me. She drove up the mountain, took one look at me and told me I had a kidney stone. 'For a man, that is as sore as it gets,' she said. Somehow we staggered to her car and started down the mountain to the nearest hospital. By now it was getting light and I thought I was dying. Then, as we drove over the crest of a hill, the morning sun lifted above the horizon and shone straight into my face. The pain disappeared. I cried aloud – this time not from agony but from astonishment.

Of course the pain came back again but this time the sun came with it. And that morning the monks had no bread.

Near Vergenoeg the water is flowing strongly over the road and the Jeep makes a wall of spray on each side as I drive through. I love it. Last year it rained so much the road was impassable, so our friends had to leave their cars in town and be ferried to the farm for the winter retreat. Since then the men from Poplar Grove come here every week to fill the furrows with stones so people don't get stuck. No need to run to the government each time we have a problem. It is our road so we look after it.

The pearl in a bowl rolls of itself
Under the scissors
Silk from a single loom

Many South Africans live insecurely here, anxious about what the future will bring. It is an uncomfortable way to live. And of course it doesn't work, this futile attempt to protect ourselves from discomfort and loss. But we also have to accept this fearfulness; it doesn't help to blame ourselves for feeling that way, creating yet another layer of suffering. When we can accept our own vulnerability we are free to dive into the aliveness of each moment and the terrors disappear by themselves. That is Zen practice. Not looking to protect ourselves but standing upright in the midst of our fears.

When the Korean Zen Master Seung Sahn was told about the Indian guru who was advising his students to flee the west coast of the United States because he predicted an earthquake there (which didn't happen), Dae Soen Sa Nim said only, 'Then who will be left to help those who are suffering?'